Vending Business

A GUIDE TO LEAPING INTO ENTREPRENEURIAL SUCCESS

ANNE M.M. PIPPEN

ISBN: 978-1-7360351-0-8

Library of Congress Control Number: 2020921719

Printed in Morrisville, North Carolina by Anne M.M. Pippen

The publisher has strived to be as accurate and complete as possible in the creation of this book.

The advice and strategies found within may not be suitable for every situation. This work is sold with the understanding that neither the author nor the publisher is held responsible for the results accrued from the advice in this book.

This book is not intended for use as a source of legal, health, medical, business, accounting, or financial advice. All readers are advised to seek the services of competent professionals in legal, health, medical, business, accounting, and financial fields.

In practical advice books, as in anything else in life, there are no guarantees of income made. Readers are cautioned to rely on their own judgment about their individual circumstances and to act accordingly.

For more information, visit https://www.VendingBusinessBook.com

For bulk book orders, contact Anne@VendingBusinessBook.com

Dedication

This book is dedicated to my daughter Erica J Pippen.
You are the best daughter a mother could want.

Learn from the past.
Live in the present.
Move toward the future.

And to my Mom, Judy Martin.
I pray that you are enjoying your afterlife.
Rest in Peace 1/20/2020

A Special Bonus Gift from Anne

Now that you have your copy of the **Vending Business Book,** you are on your way to starting a successful vending machine business. In this book, you'll discover how to avoid the pitfalls, mistakes and missteps that could slow you down or create financial challenges along with key information designed to help you prosper.

I want you to have a special bonus in addition to the material contained in this book. I created my *Vending Business Toolkit* to give you even more tools to help you succeed. It includes several Excel spreadsheets for tracking different facets of your business, a sample contract and a recommended resource list.

While this toolkit of ideas and forms is offered for sale, as a special bonus you can claim it for free here: https://www.VendingBusinessBook.com/gift

There's so much confusing information out there about starting and growing a vending machine business. I don't want you to have to go through what I did to figure it out. That's why I created this book and all the additional resource tools for you to use.

I'm in your corner. Let me know if I can help further.

Here's to a solid start to a successful vending machine business!

Best,
Anne

Table of Contents

Acknowledgments

Thank you to all of my friends and family, especially those who read through the early rough drafts. Your help and encouragement have been greatly appreciated. Amanda Barnett, without you as a sounding board, this book would have been confusing. Laura Martin-Fedich, your input was valuable not only for the suggestions you made but the important family support you provided. Erica Pippen, when it comes to family support you are wonderful, and your help with social media has been very much appreciated. Teri Rogowski and Sky Raye, having you in my author group as we work through these writing and publishing processes together has been very comforting and enabled me to know I have not been alone on this journey.

Many thanks to my book shepherd, Diana M. Needham, and my editor, Nanette Levin. Without the first, this book would have never been written. Without the second, no one would have wanted to read this book. Diana provided valuable guidance every step of the way, from refining my book idea to creating a professional book to planning and managing the marketing campaign. Given that I am a first-time author, her expertise was invaluable. Nanette provided not only editing but great guidance for arranging the content and adding humor to a subject that could be very dry and boring.

Throughout my life and career, there have been many people who have mentored and influenced me. While building my vending business, I was honored to meet and get to know several mentors. Carl

Baumann from SCORE had the most profound effect on growing my business from the beginning. He taught me the important details I wasn't taught in business school and encouraged me throughout the difficult start-up phase. David Newton, small business guy extraordinaire, helped me realize the importance of networking. Eva Ferrell has been a wonderful fount of support and understanding throughout the entire business and book experience.

I am grateful for two professional experts in the vending business, Mark Hilliard as my vending machine mover and repair person and Chuck Hilliard, an excellent machine salesperson and route procurer. Your advice, consulting, and tips are invaluable to me.

These acknowledgements would not be complete without mentioning Heidi White and her family for all of the love and encouragement given to me over the past 25 plus years. As my best friend, I appreciate the fact that you treat me and Erica like family and include us in your holiday and family celebrations. Len, Hannah, Jon, Jean, and Frank have all brightened and enlivened my life.

Introduction

"Have you finished my work yet?" my boss angrily asks, as he **finally** strolls into the office after golfing with his buddies all morning.

Some days, you just shake your head and wonder how you got here. I had spent two years more than I should have doing my boss's work for half what he was being paid. To make it worse, I was reporting to several other "bosses" and my employees weren't pulling their weight. This was adding to my already bulging workload. How did I go from a 20-year medical research scientist with an MBA and work that had been honored extensively with accolades and awards during my career to **this**? I deserved better.

Finally, I left. Part of my dream was to experience the various aspects of business operations. My prior job was financially focused, and I found this limiting. I wanted to experience what it was like to do all it takes to run a company. I must admit, it took me a while to find my stride.

Consulting sounded like a great fit because I love solving puzzles. This would also give me a more comprehensive view of business operations while putting me in an ideal position to make a big difference. The idea of guiding a business toward functioning optimally really appealed to me.

I was doing contract compliance consulting, being brought into companies to fix issues. Right, staff gets a little twitchy when they hear you're the one who's going to be telling them what they're doing wrong. Showing up for a job that made others feel nervous and defensive as they plotted to ignore my recommendations wasn't the good life I was shooting for. You learn things when you discover the people responsible for being out of compliance are the same people charged with instituting necessary changes. Frustrating, scary things.

OK, that didn't work. How about going into business for myself?

Network marketing was interesting. I learned a lot as a distributor about interacting with other people, having a positive attitude, and prospecting. Luminaries like Stephen Covey and Zig Ziglar were my guides along with the tapes I listened to every week by successful network marketing people. I was pretty good at everything except the direct sales part of the business. You can probably gather why that didn't last long.

As I pondered the possibilities for future bliss, I started to get clearer about what I wanted, or probably more accurately, what I didn't want. I considered teaching yoga and aerobics, but paying rent and utilities while recruiting students to start a business sounded too risky to me. Then it hit me.

I wanted to start a business that didn't have any bosses or employees or overhead. Crazy, right? I looked into various franchises like Kumon, which offers tutoring to children, and Camp Bow Wow which is a boarding place for dogs. Both of these options would fit with my personality and strengths; however, the initial investment was too high for me. I would have to hire employees, and I would need to rent space. I wanted to stay away from those headaches.

When trying to find the best business for me, I searched through everything I could find at the time. My primary search was for independently operated businesses. This brought me to a list of the best self-run businesses. I eliminated options such as tax preparation, website design, technology repair & IT support, personal training, real estate broker, and a host of others for various reasons.

Then I came across the small business idea of vending machine operator. Who would have thought that vending machines were managed by small business owners? What I discovered is vending machines are a totally separate business from where they're located. These are owned, maintained, and operated by independent companies, mostly small ones.

Why do I get into my history of job fails just prior to finding the vending machine industry? Because I think we've all been there. Most people won't admit their mistakes, but I'm going to share some doozies with you as part of this book; my gift to you.

By now you've probably guessed I didn't leap into the vending machine industry and find instantaneous success. With the benefit of hindsight, though, I can guide you through what's it's taken me ten years to learn. I really wish that I'd had a book like this to read before I got started. It would have saved me a lot of time and money.

I've been where you might be in a high stress job but scared to plunge into the unknown world of business startup. If you've ever considered leaving the corporate rat race for a more peaceful, fulfilling, and independent lifestyle, this is the book for you.

Inside you will discover how to:

- Decide if a vending business is right for you
- Set up your business the right way
- Choose the right vending machine equipment
- Obtain optimal locations
- Source the best-selling vending machine products at the best price
- Provide great service
- Grow, expand, and scale

I've also included a look inside a day in the life of a successful vending machine operator and some unique concerns that have surfaced from the current pandemic situation. I've even created some bonus materials to help you with building your own business. Just check out my website at https://www.VendingBusinessBook.com/gift.

Now if you are like me, you'll probably want to skip to what sounds like the most interesting chapters. Not to sound like your mother, but I seriously mean it when I suggest you do what I say, not what I do. Unless, of course, you want to spend a couple of years staring at a chunk of your retirement savings gathering dust in your garage (more on that later).

If you are exploring starting a vending machine business and looking for key insights to help you decide, read this book in the order it is written. Each chapter builds upon the previous one. If you already have a vending business and are looking for tips on how to grow your company or solve specific challenges, feel free to go directly to the chapters that provide the information you need.

I understand what it's like to struggle to find a job that makes you happy and fulfilled. I share my story here and in the following pages to illustrate to you that my path wasn't a straight one to vending machine business owner success. You'll find a lot of information on what not to do, because, well, I guess I'm kind of prone to learning the hard way. Of course, I'll also share best practices based on considerable experience that's led me to better solutions.

If you feel like you're never going to find the right job for you, have hope. I can now say, after a decade getting to a place where I'm running a successful venture in this industry, I've found the secret to a happy balance for me with a business that offers the freedom and flexibility to choose how I want to live my life. I hope you can too.

CHAPTER 1

So, You Think You Want to Start a Vending Machine Business?

I never imagined there was so much to learn about vending machines. Over the past ten years I've discovered things I never thought I'd want to know but have come to appreciate. Most people assume vending machines are owned by the facility where they're located or are managed by huge companies. That's not how the business works. The routes are owned by people like you and me.

If you're thinking about starting your own small business, this industry has a lot of opportunities. It offers flexible hours, relatively low startup costs, lots of choice on your route size and employee count, low overhead, and many different activities during your week. Like any business, it requires weekly maintenance in the form of customer service and marketing, but once you set it up with systems, it gets easier. What I provide in this book will help you create better strategies to get to your goals faster.

It took me a while to find vending machine operation as a business venture, but now ten years in, I know it's the right business for me. Hopefully, you'll see the same things I did that make it so appealing. That doesn't mean I didn't make mistakes starting out.

My decision to initially focus on health foods was a major misstep. You learn to focus on what people do, not what they say in this business. I think people believe they're going to practice good habits when smart choices are made available, but the fact is, most vending machine habits gravitate toward vice.

There are a lot of reasons a vending machine business might not be right for you. There's heavy lifting, a constant need for marketing (locations change or leave), and a need to be attentive about keeping machines stocked and working. But there's also a variety to your day and independence this business provides that's hard to match with other ventures.

Before you set out on the path toward becoming a vending machine operator, think about what appeals to you. That will help you decide if this business is right for you. I'll help you discover important questions to ask while laying out a plan for success if you do decide to go this route. Of course, lessons learned the hard way are sometimes the best teachers. You'll be able to avoid some of the mistakes I made with what I share in the following pages.

Vending Machine Curiosities

Vending machines have been around for a long time. The diversity of options and curious beginnings can be fascinating. If you're going to be in this business, it's good to know some of the history and also what the business looks like today.

Did you know that the first American vending machine sold gum? I discovered this fun fact while researching for this book. Today you can sell just about anything in a vending machine. You have probably noticed the vending machines selling electronic supplies when you're at the airport. Carvana is a vending machine that sells cars. You can sell coffee, ice cream, sandwiches, toys . . . the list of options is almost endless.

Personally, I don't want to sell cars in a vending machine because the investment is too high. That's something to consider when deciding what type of vending you want to do. Costs aren't always obvious.

Would you believe over 50% of vending machines are placed in offices or manufacturing buildings? Consider if that's something that matters to you. I have machines in nursing homes, schools, fire stations, and many other types of locations. There's a big variety of places you can choose from as you build your route.

One thing I think is important about machine location is that you need to diversify. If I had all of my machines in schools when the COVID-19 pandemic closed them unexpectedly, I would have been in horrible trouble. Thankfully, I had some machines in essential locations so I could afford to eat, pay rent, you know, stay alive.

I was surprised to discover cold drinks make up over 30% of vending sales. This is good news. Cold drinks are easy. If you choose this type of machine, know cans have a longer shelf life than bottles. Even cold drink bottles, though, have a longer shelf life than most snacks. Expiration dates will become an important thing to consider and keep track of as you venture into this industry.

The National Automatic Merchandising Association (NAMA) states there are over 5 million vending machines in the US.[1] That number will surely increase as the population and number of businesses increase. Today, more than ever, as the world population starts to consider more opportunities to work from home, vending machine businesses are becoming an attractive alternative to desk jobs.

Things to Consider on Vending Machine Choice

There are lots of different reasons to choose or avoid certain types of products in this business. Maintenance costs vary a great deal. Some machines are more costly or labor intensive to service than others. All have hidden minimum costs to keep them running. Certain items won't sell in the location you've chosen. Some things won't sell anywhere.

For example, I started off with the wrong product focus and had to reinvest to start over after discovering logic doesn't necessarily play a role in behavior. Since I was a health nut and thought healthy vending was the wave of the future, I invested in five vending machines for healthy foods.

The company I chose to purchase machines from offered training for everyone who invested. This was an appealing perk since I didn't have much knowledge of the business. It was a deciding factor in selecting their machines. I attended the training weekend and started my own business immediately after flying across the country for this education. As you will find out later in the book, this wasn't the best way to start.

Something else to keep in mind is there are hidden costs in operating vending machines. Everyone thinks of initial purchase price, product replacement, and probably figures there will be maintenance costs to keep the machines running, but many don't consider the little things.

For example, in snack machines, you have to keep at least $30 in coins for the coin mechanism to work correctly. The snack rows need to be kept filled to the level needed at your location, which usually means weekly or bi-weekly trips that cost gas, merchandise inventory, and time. All of that is your continuing investment in the machine and your business.

Sandwich machines have a fast turnover since the product expires so quickly. This means that you have to service the machine more frequently than you would a standard snack machine. This also means more trips to the store to purchase the sandwiches.

Coffee machines are messy, so you have to clean them more frequently and carry more cleaning supplies with you to sweep up coffee grounds. It's also more work to clean the inside of the machine.

Thinking About Your Priorities

My reasons for choosing a vending machine business were pretty simple. I didn't want to have to manage human employees. My employees are the machines. I wanted to be my own boss. This pretty much assured I wouldn't grow to hate my boss as had been the case in the past. This industry allows you to make your own hours. That was an important consideration for me. A big bonus was the flexibility, simplicity, and scalability this type of venture provides. It gives me the freedom to spend time doing the things I want.

As far as the initial investment is concerned, startup costs for vending businesses can vary a great deal, allowing you to make decisions on the amount you want to invest. If you only have $500 to begin with, you can purchase a used snack or drink vending machine. Alternatively, you can purchase a few bulk vending machines which are the little gum, candy, and toy machines you often see at the entryway of grocery stores or in hair salons. They're the ones where you insert a quarter or quarters into a slot, turn the knob and get some skittles.

If you have $100,000 to invest, you can purchase someone else's route and have a bunch of productive machines right out of the gate. It's an easier way to start that will get you going with a lot less time, but not everyone can afford to do that.

Lifting and traveling is part of almost any vending machine operation, but the machines and geographical area you choose can make a big difference in how much of this is necessary. If you're selling perishable items, storage between and during route filling times is something you need to think about.

In the following chapters, I'll walk you through some of the most basic things you need to know to be successful. In addition, I'll help you get a good handle on more complicated aspects of the business. I'll also share what I learned along the way. This is your step-by-step guide to building a vending machine business on your own. If you'd prefer to have a mentor who can help you move forward faster supporting you, I can do that too. Either way, you'll want to grab my free bonus gift before you dig in at https://www.VendingBusinessBook.com/gift.

I hope you'll find your vending machine business to be as rewarding as I have mine.

CHAPTER 2

Decide: Asking the Right
Questions with Goals and Strategies

It was a treat when my machines were delivered! Seeing these big and beautiful machines being unloaded from the truck and put in my garage was physical evidence that my vending machine operator business was a real thing. By this time, I had also received my business cards which were so pretty.

Too bad I didn't have any locations for those five machines. It took me months of attending networking groups, cold calling businesses, starting a website, and yes, panicking that this business would never amount to anything. This was after emptying my 403B and putting in countless hours, sweat, and tears.

Finally, I hit gold. I cold-called a location and when I asked if they needed a vending machine at their location, I found out that their current vendor wanted to get out of the business. She was selling her machines. I contacted the woman, toured her route of three machines, made sure that all of her machines worked and learned how to work them, and purchased her route. I still hadn't placed my five machines, but finally my business was out of the starting gate. This felt wonderful!

By this time, I was attending networking groups all over the area, five days a week. This gave me the opportunity to perfect my elevator pitch, which is what you tell someone about your business when you have 30 seconds or less to explain. I also got to know some great people who gave me great advice on how to move forward. One such piece of advice was to attend the free small business workshops at the area colleges.

At one of the workshops, I met a man who volunteered with SCORE. He helped me write my business plan. Who knew that a business plan would help your business grow? Yeah, my MBA didn't cover this.

SCORE is a volunteer organization that consists of mostly retired businesspeople who want to help new business owners get up and running. "For over 50 years SCORE has served as America's premier source of free business mentoring and education. As a resource partner of the U.S. Small Business Administration (SBA), SCORE has helped more than 11 million entrepreneurs through mentoring, workshops, and educational resources since 1964."[2]

Besides learning about the necessity of a business plan from my SCORE mentor, I discovered the importance of having a website, and developing a good practice of listing and updating my business on a lot of online business media sites. Establishing a social media presence and creating a website can really help your marketing take off.

I had no experience with social media or websites, so I hired someone to do all of this for me. I think it was $500 well spent. My web designer helped me become the number one Google search result for vending in our area. This lasted a year, then I forgot to renew my domain and lost the site. As you can tell, I still don't have much of an understanding of the online world and websites. I tried for about a year to get a new site up on my own but couldn't figure it out. Then I realized that I didn't need to have all of the bells and whistles and set up a basic site with two pages. One page telling what and who I am, and one with a contact sheet for people to fill out.

Eventually, I met an operations manager at one of the networking groups who needed vending machines at five of her locations. I finally placed my five health conscious machines! I was flying high. So, when one of the people who I had met at the three-day training seminar called me and told me he was getting out of the business and asked if I would like to purchase four of his vending machines, I jumped at the opportunity. I found four more locations fairly quickly. With twelve total locations, I was feeling like a real businesswoman.

Then, one of the locations called and said they were going with their corporation's vending machines and asked if I would please take mine out. What a downer. I took out that machine and it sat in my garage for a couple months before I found another location. I felt like quitting. Things weren't going so well. *This is hard. I'm not making enough money.*

The problem with that sort of thinking is that it is hard to change. However, if you have a schedule, read positive books, and work your plan (business plan and networking groups), eventually you will become a more positive person.

Understanding what's important to you is a critical first step before you start to consider if a vending machine business might be right for you. While there are a lot of different specialized opportunities ranging from snacks to cars, there are certain lifestyle realities this type of business brings that may or may not fit your dreams. If you do decide this is right for you, knowing where you want to go will help you determine what type of product best fits your priorities.

What are your goals? This is an important insight that will help you decide if a vending business is what you want to do. Your business has to be able to help you reach your goals. That's a no brainer. Why would you start a business that didn't give you anything back? You probably wouldn't take a vacation without any maps, GPS tools, or an idea of where you want to go. Goals act like a road map for your life.

They help you take control and guide you along your journey so that your experiences are rich, satisfying, and enjoyable.

Answer these questions to find out if the vending machine business is right for you. If you answer yes to all, you are good to go:

- Do you have reliable transportation to get from place to place to restock machines?
- Are you willing to work to be profitable within 3 to 5 years?
- Do you want a flexible schedule?
- Can you lift and carry the heavy products (up to 40 pounds)?
- Do you like driving and meeting new people?
- Do you have good people skills or are you willing to make the effort to acquire these skills?
- Are you willing to keep the machines clean and organized?
- Do you have other sources of income so you can live without a steady paycheck until your new business turns a profit?

Goals give you focus. Think again about driving without having a destination in mind. You may end up in the middle of the frozen tundra. This is a literal example of what life is like without a goal or destination in mind. It's pointless and a waste of energy and effort. You can have all the potential in the world, but without focus, your abilities and talents are useless. This sense of direction is what allows your mind to focus on a target. Rather than wasting energy driving aimlessly, an objective allows you to arrive at your destination and reach your goal.

I think Zig Ziglar said it best, "If you aim at nothing, you will hit it every time."[3]

Setting Smart Goals

Goals allow you to measure progress. By setting goals for yourself you are able to focus on a fixed endpoint or benchmark to measure your progress. Take this scenario for example: When I first started my vending machine business, I didn't set goals for how quickly I'd place machines, how much money I wanted to earn, or how much traffic I wanted at the locations. Consequently, five new machines that cost me $35,000 sat in my garage for fourteen months earning nothing. Once I stepped back and created a business plan with this information mapped out and started marketing consistently, I was able to increase my revenue by $30,000 within two years. If I had done that to begin with, I would have saved a lot of time and anxiety.

Goals keep you undistracted. By setting goals, you give yourself mental boundaries. When you have a certain endpoint in mind, you automatically stay away from certain distractions and stay focused on the goal. This process happens subtly.

A good way to start figuring out what your goals are is to set "SMART goals." There are variations of what SMART stands for, but in essence, goals should be:

- Specific - What are you precisely trying to change/do? What behaviors will get you the results you want?
- Measurable - How are you going to count and track progress?
- Attainable - Do you have any knowledge or skill gaps that could prevent you from achieving your goals? What research do you need to do to ensure you are equipped to achieve your goals?
- Relevant - Is your goal useful to your life? What will you gain by achieving this goal? Does it reflect your values and help you achieve long-term objectives?
- Time bound - How much time is necessary to reach your goal? You'll want to document what you want to achieve and by when as part of this process.

To demonstrate, I'm going to share some of my big SMART goals from the beginning of my independent business owner life. When I first decided to go into business for myself, I needed to focus on the switch from a corporate mindset to an independent business owner attitude. But that wasn't the biggest challenge; I needed an understanding of the vending machine industry to ensure my goals were attainable. Of course, not to be deterred, I set SMART goals anyway.

- Specific - Establish a ten machine $50,000 route in 12 months' time that fosters healthy eating in central North Carolina with good-for-you food as the only option from my machines. This will brand the company as the premiere healthy vending machine firm in the state focused exclusively on healthy snacks and beverages. By year two, locations will be chasing me down to replace existing provider's unhealthy machines with my superior solution.

- Measurable - Identify ideal locations in the central North Carolina area for my healthy vending machines. From that list, schedule 100 visits in the first three months of operations (industry norms state it takes ten prospect calls to generate one possible sale). Schedule five calls on Monday, Wednesday and Friday of every week for the first three months of operations. This will produce a waiting list of locations by the end of month. Ten businesses will happily grab the coveted spot of being serviced by my company with healthy vending food. Purchase five more machines in month four with the tremendous profits from the first five machines. Have a qualifying competition for all the locations now on the waiting list, which is growing every day with word-of-mouth excitement spreading and sending referrals my way.

- Attainable - I went to training and bought five machines so now I can accomplish anything by simply dreaming it in my sleep. So, sure, these easy goals are attainable.

- Relevant - I want to be healthy so know everyone else does. As the first exclusively healthy vending machine operator in the state, I'm appealing to everyone's deep, unmet need while fulfilling a passion of mine. This is a win-win as people will immediately shun unhealthy snacks and embrace my ideal of converting every machine in the state to good-for-you food only. My easy-to-achieve plan for prospecting is ideally suited for this aim.

- Time bound - Solicit 50 locations within the first month to find homes for my first five machines. Place all machines in thriving locations within 30 days of delivery to my garage. Spend month two and three securing locations for the next five machines and getting prepared to handle the onslaught of demand for my company's offerings. Start blocking off three hours per week for the growing number of media interview requests seeking me as an authority and innovator in the vending machine space. Plan for a year-two quadruple demand but settle on twenty machines in locations that will never change as the final strategy for my personal comfort and great retirement wealth. This is achieved by the beginning of year two due to all the word-of-mouth referral business coming in.

OK, maybe that wasn't my actual SMART goal document when I started out, but it sure reflects what I was thinking. In time, reality set in, prompting me to focus my time on learning about the industry and business operations in general. I learned a lot that I hadn't previously considered – or realized was important.

After too much time staring at my retirement savings gathering dust in my garage, I got smarter with my plan. One thing I learned was I needed to have about 50 machines to make a living wage. That's because most of the machines you place won't generate sufficient revenue. It's the 80/20 rule, or Pareto's Principle. Twenty percent of your locations will produce 80% of your profits.

At the year two mark, I had 25 machines placed. I really needed double that to cover my living expenses. By this point, I had a website up and going and was handing out business cards, attending networking meetings and encouraging referrals from existing customers. About that time, I also realized you could buy routes from other people. I thought that 3 machine route was a fluke.

Boy, did my SMART goals change with the knowledge I had gained! Here's what my SMART goals looked like a couple of years into my business venture (oh, and you could actually use these as guideposts for your particular venture, which is not something I'd recommend you do with my first set of SMART goals):

- Specific - Establish enough vending machine income to pay all living expenses plus 20% additional profit to go toward my retirement fund within the next 48 months.

- Measurable - Increase business by 25 machines in the next two years. Transition product mix to 80% junk food (normal vending machine fare – by now I had realized why I didn't have any competition in the healthy food only vending offerings) and 20% healthy. Move away from specialization on smaller office buildings and put a new emphasis on manufacturing plants and hub locations by transitioning 50% of current route to these preferred locations. Put higher focus on buying routes vs. establishing new ones with a goal of securing 60% of new business by purchasing existing businesses.

- Attainable - With increased knowledge of the industry and more realistic expectations that include putting more skin in the game, these goals are a little bit of a reach, but most certainly doable in the timeframe outlined.

- Relevant - In reassessing my true aim, I realized my primary business objectives were about lifestyle and income priorities. Once I realigned my business activities with a more practical vision, it was easy to see – and get enthusiastic about doing – what I needed to accomplish to reach income objectives.

- Time Bound - These SMART goals are to be implemented and completed within the next two years. The details of how this will be accomplished are laid out in an Excel spreadsheet.

As you can see, my SMART goals changed a lot with experience. Would it have been better for me to fully research the industry before I jumped in headlong with a flight out west and a $35,000 machine purchase? Sure, it would have. But that's not usually how life goes. I believed what I was sold by people and a company who, understandably, were most interested in getting my business.

We all tend to get excited about something we hear and leap in thinking there will be nothing to it as we get mesmerized by the hype. The good news is, creating the right kind of goals can help you a lot toward business success. Just don't beat yourself up if you have a shaky start. That's normal. I did it too. Of course, one of my major goals in writing this book is to give you the right kind of information so that you don't have to learn the hard way. Cocky and stubborn can get expensive. I know.

Goals help you overcome procrastination. When you set a goal for yourself you make yourself accountable to finish the task. This is in complete contrast with when you do things based off a whim where you don't care if you complete them or not. Of course, it's also important to learn about industry norms and your market constraints so you don't get frustrated with goals that aren't realistic or attainable.

Goals tend to stick in your mind, and if not completed, they give you a slap in the back of your head reminder. These reminders in the back of your head help you to combat laziness, provided you don't get frustrated by reaching too high at first. There's a happy medium between far-fetched and too easy. You want to set goals you can meet that are a little bit of a stretch. Note the difference between my initial SMART expectations and my grounded strategies two years later.

Goals give you motivation. The root of all the motivation or inspiration you have ever felt in your entire life is goals. Goal setting provides you the foundation for your drive. By making a goal, you give yourself a concrete endpoint to aim for and get excited about. It gives you something to focus on and put 100% of your effort into. Goals are simply tools to focus your energy in positive directions. These can be changed as your priorities change, new ones are added, and others are dropped.

To accomplish your goals, you need to know how to set them. There are four golden rules that can help you do this. Step one of these is to set goals that genuinely motivate you. Try to imagine working day in and day out toward a goal that doesn't excite you very much. That doesn't sound very fun. If something isn't very important to you, chances are you will give up before you succeed. When you think about setting a goal, take time to analyze why it is so meaningful to you. If you are not truly excited about it, then it's probably not worth pursuing.

Step two is to create an action plan. Once you have your primary smart goals, you can break them down into smaller goals. For instance, if your primary goal is to be accomplished in five years, what do you need to accomplish in the first year? Goals work best because you can evaluate your progress objectively.

The physical act of putting your goals into writing makes them tangible and real. They feel important. When you write your goals down, use words like, "I will" instead of "I might" or "I would like to." The words "I will" show power and intention. You have set yourself on a mission and speak as though you intend to accomplish it.

Step three is to carry out the plan. By writing out individual steps and crossing each one off as you complete it, you will realize the progress you are making toward your ultimate goal. This is especially important if your goal is big and demanding or will take a long time to accomplish.

Step four is to stick with the plan. Goal setting is an ongoing activity not just a means to an end. Set reminders to keep yourself on track and make time to review your goals regularly.

After setting goals, it is wise to then decide if a vending machine business will satisfy them. Setting your intentions is important in determining how you want to meet your goals. Why do you want to start a vending business? Is it because you want to work for yourself? I asked myself that question. What did I want? After having such a miserable job with too many bosses and too many employees both ripping into me with every imagined and unimagined problem, I wanted a business with no boss and no employees.

My goal was to own my own business, have low startup costs, shoulder little to no overhead, and enjoy a lot of flexibility. Most businesses require you to hire employees, so I had to search for businesses that would fit in my life that didn't demand the hiring of employees. There were several businesses I could have started that don't have any bosses or employees; however, many would require me to be on the computer all the time. Being on the computer all the time didn't interest me. I wanted a more active, social, and physical business.

Aligning Your Goals with a Vending Machine Business

Knowing your goals is important in making sure you are starting the right business. It also helps keep you on track when the going gets tough. The process I recommend you follow involves setting realistic goals. Some people might have a goal to make a lot of money without putting much work and time into their business. I don't know of any businesses that works that way. I did know someone, though, who started a vending machine business, then within a month decided he didn't make enough money, so quit. Another person started a vending business and wanted to start spending money before any money started coming in. Needless to say, this person did not stay in the business either.

Another very valid reason for starting a vending machine business is to escape from an office. I liked this idea because I don't like to be stationary and prefer moving around both inside and outside. The vending work is done from the home. This doesn't mean that you stay at home the entire time. You have to drive to your locations to fill and service your machines on a regular basis. However, you don't need an office. You use your car for servicing your route and use your home for the accounting and paperwork side of things.

Having flexible hours was also one of my goals and is a very good reason to start a vending business. Most locations are open weekdays, so most people work Monday through Friday, however, some locations are open weekends and evenings. You get to determine the days you want to work. I tend to work Monday through Friday, but if I want to take a day off during the week, I can make up that work on the weekend. In general, I spend the first part of my day driving around to service different locations and the later part of the day taking care of the accounting and paperwork part of the business.

Another great opportunity while working a vending business is interaction with others. Machine locations are filled with people who are happy to see you since you are bringing them food and drink. At most of my locations people get excited to see the "Snack Lady." My locations also vary in type, so I meet people from all walks of life. I have a paving company, vet office, manufacturing company, gene therapy laboratory, government office, a school, and a good number of other location types. Getting to know the people at these various locations helps keep me well-rounded and is very rewarding. I don't see the same people day in and day out, and every day I hear different stories and see different interactions. While visiting different locations, people may ask you for special requests or just want to talk. It is always good business to build strong relationships with the people.

More control over your financial future is one of the best parts of the vending business. You can build your business as big or keep it as small as you want. Since I didn't want to hire employees, I knew I was limiting the size of my business. At the time, all I wanted was to make enough money to support myself. My bills were relatively few, just car payment, rent, electric, Internet, and food. After working the business for a while, I figured out that the highest number of machines I could handle by myself was between 50 and 70.

If you want to grow more, just hire employees to help you out. The employees that you hire can run the route for you, or if you like running the route, they can manage the paperwork.

You can divide the work up however you would like. After making that decision, the sky is the limit. Grow as big as you want. Growth takes a lot of work, but you are not hindered in your success. You do not have to rely on a boss to give you a raise or promotion, you give yourself one by working harder and smarter.

CHAPTER 3

Start

You don't have to know everything before you start! If you wait to learn everything first, you will never start. You need to give yourself permission to start. Don't worry about what others will think, or what the negative side of your brain is telling you. Figure out what your goal is and work toward it.

At a fairly young age, I learned that you can't know everything before you start something. My parents signed me up for piano lessons. I never wanted to go to the lessons because I didn't know how to play the piano very well. When the instructor corrected me on anything: posture, notes, keys, I hated it. I wanted to be perfect before I learned how to play.

I practiced all of the time. I even got up in the middle of dinner to play and practice, but I wasn't perfect. I put up with the lessons, or should I say my parents put up with my complaining about the lessons, until my teacher said she couldn't help me anymore; I needed to go to a more advanced teacher. Thankfully (at the time), the new instructor was more expensive, so when I complained to my parents, they let me stop. I have regretted not taking the time to learn how to play better. Now, I realize that everyone who is good at the piano has had to learn a lot and that no one is perfect from the start. Just think what would happen if everyone waited to be perfect before they performed. There would be no music in the world.

There are more than 28 million small businesses in the United States, making up a whopping 99.7 percent of all U.S. businesses, according to the Small Business Administration.[4] When you consider some of the most popular reasons to start a business—including having a unique business idea, designing a career that has the flexibility to grow with you, working toward financial independence, and investing in yourself—it's no wonder that small businesses are everywhere.

Once I decided to start a vending machine business, I figured that with my MBA I knew everything there was to know about business. That wasn't true; I had no clue how to start. So, I looked for vending machine companies that offered training on how to run a vending machine business. I found a few such companies and weeded through those by deleting the franchises.

Next, I called the two remaining companies. One of those companies was more helpful, responding to all of my questions. They even gave me the contact information of people who had used their training so I could call them to ask about their experience. I called those people and received glowing recommendations. That made the decision to choose them easy for both training and the purchase of my first five vending machines. As an aside, those people who I called to ask about the company had been plants; they were paid by the vending machine company. Of course, I didn't find that out until long after I had invested heavily. I learned the hard way to be more rigorous with my research when making these kinds of decisions.

Not every small business is positioned for success. According to data from the U.S. Bureau of Labor Statistics, about 20 percent of small businesses fail within their first year. By the end of their fifth year, roughly 50 percent of small businesses fail. After 10 years, the survival rate drops to approximately 35 percent.[5] So, you may be in for a real challenge when you decide to take the plunge, ditch your day job, and become a business owner.

Setting the foundation for success is something you personally need to do; a mentor can guide you, but you have to do the work. No one will have the same desire to succeed that you do. If you hire someone to get you started in the business, it will not be set up the way you want it. You will miss all of the growth in both your personal and business life that comes from learning along the way.

If you do not want the experience of growing your own business, you could look for a job. Alternatively, you could perhaps partner with someone else whose brilliance is setting up businesses so you can focus on your unique talents.

The most important step to get this business started is to start it. Don't get me wrong, there are critical items that need to be in place so that you don't get in trouble with your new locations or the government. Here are some ideas to consider:

Goals

In the last chapter, we addressed the need to set your goals. One mistake that startups make is to skip the planning phase. Planning may be tedious, but without a solid plan for your business that includes business idea research and market potential, you will be operating in the dark. SMART goals designed specifically for your business can give you direction when you first start out, then keep you on track during the day-to-day operations. By making sure your goals are SMART, you can identify where you want to go and outline specific steps that you will take to get there.

The most important plans to consider include creating a business plan with particular attention to the financial and marketing plan portions of this document.

Business Plan

After you have made your decision to start a vending machine business, your next step is to create a business plan. A business plan is a blueprint that will guide your business from the start-up phase through refinement, and eventually into business growth. It is a must-have for all new businesses. The good news is there are different types of business plans for different types of businesses. Some can be very short.

If you intend to seek financial support from an investor or financial institution, a traditional business plan is a must. This type of business plan is generally long and thorough. It has a common set of sections that investors and banks look for when they are evaluating your idea.

If you don't anticipate seeking financial support, a simple one-page business plan can give you clarity about what you hope to achieve and how you plan to do it. In fact, you can even create a working business plan on a single sheet of paper and improve it over time. Some kind of plan in writing is always better than nothing.

If you're going to do a quickie business plan, the most important areas to focus on are the marketing and money aspects. You want to have at least a rough plan of how you're going to promote your venture. What's unusual with vending machine businesses is you're not marketing to the end user. The person you want to impress is the one who makes the decision about allowing your machine to be placed at their location. Think about what might be important to those controlling your ideal locations.

On the money side, it's wise to at least have a sense about your projected expenses and income. Predict higher than you think on the cost side and a bit lower on the income front. A good rule of thumb for predicting the next year's sales is to increase the present years sales by 15%.

Most of your expenses with a vending machine business will be fixed costs, so those are pretty easy to calculate. Variable costs are frequently tied to additional profit, with margins on food and beverage machines generally in the 50-60% range. Many Small Business Development Centers (SBDCs) have income and expense projection calculators built into their business plan templates. Consider reaching out to an advisor at your local SBDC for free support in crafting your business plan if you're getting confused with projections.

You can get support from many different avenues when writing your business plan. The one I chose was SCORE. SCORE is an organization that offers free counseling to small business startups. I signed up for SCORE and was given a great mentor who walked me through the business plan steps and gave advice and critique.

The basic steps of a business plan include an executive summary, which is an overview of your business and your plans. It comes first in your plan and is ideally only one or two pages. Think about what you want to focus on with your product and location over the next five years here. How many machines do you want to be managing at what type of facilities? Are employees in your future? Consider a strategy that includes a diverse mix of machine placements so you can more easily weather economic and other unexpected challenges.

Next is the opportunity section, which answers these questions: "What are you actually selling?" and "How are you solving a problem or need for your market?" "Who is your target market and competition?" This is where you want to do some research to ensure your choice of product and location is going to be a good fit with your personal goals and also feasible in your particular vending machine market.

The third step is execution. In this part of your business plan, you will answer the question of "How you are going to take your opportunity and turn it into a business?" This section will cover your marketing and sales plan, operations, and your milestones and metrics for success. See Chapter 5 for ideas on selecting the right vending machine equipment for you, Chapter 6 and 7 on sourcing locations, and Chapter 8 on product opportunities.

The next section includes the company and management summary. Provide a quick overview of your legal structure, location, and history if you're already up and running. This is also where you'd want to mention key existing or anticipated employees.

The last part of your business plan is the financial plan, which includes a sales forecast, cash flow statement, income statement (also called profit and loss), and your balance sheet. If you need space for product images or additional information, make an appendix.

Financing Options

After you have your business plan under control, you need to plan your finances. Starting a vending machine business doesn't have to require a lot of money, but it will involve some initial investment as well as the ability to cover ongoing expenses before you are turning a profit.

Put together a spreadsheet that estimates the one-time startup costs for your business (licenses and permits, equipment, inventory, legal fees, insurance, branding, market research, inventory, trademarking, etc.). You'll also want to include what you anticipate you will need to keep your business running for at least 12 months (rent, utilities, marketing and advertising, inventory, supplies, travel expenses, employee salaries, your own salary, etc.). These numbers combined are the initial investment required.

This is fairly easy to do using any spreadsheet you have available to you. I started with an Excel spreadsheet. In North Carolina, we don't need to have permits, so that cost was zero. I purchased the initial five machines, which cost roughly $35,000. I signed up for Legal Shield, which costs $40 per month. Insurance was initially $35 per month. Inventory cost around $4,000 because of the product variety and the coinage needed. In order for the machine to work and take dollars and coins, you need to start with about $30 in nickels, dimes, and quarters. My initial startup cost was roughly $40,000. I don't recommend purchasing the machines before you have the locations. Of course, I did, so I hope now that you're reading this book, you'll take heed and benefit from one of the many lessons I learned the hard way.

My projected costs for the first year were naïvely estimated. I didn't have my first five machines placed. However, my goal was to have 10 machines within the first year. So, another $35,000 for machines, $480 for legal, and $420 for insurance. Inventory costs would decrease after the initial investment of $24,000 for the year and $300 for coinage. My first year estimated costs were roughly $60,000.

Now that you have rough figures in mind, there are a number of ways you can finance your small business, including:

Financing using small business loans – You can ask a bank for funds if you have another established business with collateral and strong credit. Traditional banks are a great starting point and can help you figure out where you stand in terms of qualifying for funding. Even if your business doesn't have a strong enough track record or enough assets as collateral to qualify for a bank loan, talking to someone at a traditional bank can help you figure out what documents you need and what your best options may be.

Locally owned banks, in particular, are a great resource for small businesses because they often have a strong interest in economic development in the community. In the third quarter of 2016, the Federal Deposit Insurance Corp. found that 43% of small loans to businesses came from community banks.[6]

Applying for loans using the small business administration (SBA) – This is for businesses who don't meet traditional banks' strict lending criteria. The U.S. Small Business Administration (SBA) offers lenders, mostly traditional banks, a federal guarantee on your loan. This makes it less risky for banks to lend you the funds you need to be successful. In guaranteeing the loans, the SBA also connects you with favorable rates offered by traditional lenders. And unlike most bank loans, you can use an SBA loan to start a business.

However, the application process isn't easy, and you can find yourself trapped under a heap of documents while you work through the appropriate forms. Online lender SmartBiz provides a more streamlined SBA application process, originating SBA loans faster than traditional banks.[7]

Requesting a loan online – This is for people with personal credit that is not very good, who want fast funding or an easier application process. Warning, the interest rates will be higher. Because traditional banks limit their loans, online lenders have seen an increase in popularity. A report by Morgan Stanley predicts they'll provide 16% of small-business loans by 2020.[8] Online lenders are particularly useful for owners struggling with bad credit or those in need of fast cash. Several of them are able to turn around funding within 24 hours.

Requesting crowd funding, such as "GoFundMe." Crowd funding is generally a request for donors (sometimes with a promise to deliver some kind of product or service based on the amount they give, but not always) to help fund a cause, project, initiative, medical challenge, etc. Most crowd funding sites charge somewhere around a 5% platform charge. The hosting sites don't loan any money. They simply process payments from (usually) the general public to support a request.

Applying for Small Business grants – These grants are free financing and offer a way for business owners to get established or grow, without having to worry about paying back the money. Typically offered through nonprofits, foundations, government agencies, and corporations, some grants focus on specific types of business owners, such as minorities, veterans, and women. Grants for small business owners aren't as easy to find, but they are out there. For a vending machine business, you can also check with your city or state government to see if they're aware of any local, regional, or federal grants available in the area.

Here are a few links to help you find more information about grant opportunities:

https://www.sba.gov/funding-programs/grants/grants-programs-eligibility
https://www.nerdwallet.com/article/small-business/small-business-grants

The downside to free financing is that everybody wants it. It will take a lot of work to find and apply for grants, but time spent searching for free money opportunities could pay off in the long run.

Using Credit Unions loans – Credit unions have increased their small-business loans by 60% since 2008, according to the National Association of Federal Credit Unions.[9] You'll likely have to be a member. But, the co-op nature of credit unions often ties them to the community, so you may also gain the benefits of more personal relationships and name recognition. As some say, it's who you know…

You can also attempt to get your business off the ground by not taking any loans or by using as little startup capital as possible. A combination of the paths listed above work best. The goal here, though, is to work through the options and create a plan for setting up the capital you need to get your business off the ground.

There are two basic ways, financially speaking, to start a vending business without a loan or grant. One is to have enough savings so that you can manage for 6-12 months while you build your business. The second is to continue working your present job until your business can sustain you. This is a very personal decision; there are considerations for all decisions.

If you decide to start a vending business without any distractions like work, you will probably grow faster. This makes sense: fewer distractions allow you to concentrate and do more. To start a business this way, you can take a few different routes. You can take out a business loan for enough to build the business and support yourself. If you have a 401K or 403B, you can set up a C-corp, so your retirement plan holds 95% or less of the stock. If you have a person who can support you, you can start your business with just the money needed to purchase the machines and product.

If you decide to keep working while you build your business, you run the risk of not being able to service your locations in a timely fashion. Growth will be slower. You will also have more difficulty setting up appointments for new locations since most of your new locations will want you to come in during normal business hours. The initial set up of a location takes anywhere from three to eight hours, depending on the number of machines you need to set up. If I need to set up one machine, I allow 3 hours. If I have two machines to set up, I allow 4 hours. The advantage of working while building your business is that you will not need to take out loans, dip into your 401K, or have someone support you.

This brings us to the decision of how you want to grow your business. While choosing the way you want to grow, consider your circumstances, startup capital, goals, and loans (short term or equipment financing costs). You can build it yourself, which is the cheapest and takes the most time. Or, you can purchase an existing vending machine route, which is the fastest way to start, but the equipment will be used, and contracts with locations might be near the end.

You can also buy into a franchise or business opportunity. With this approach there is often training available; however, the capital investment is higher, and you have to pay a percentage of your profits.

There are a couple different types of franchises you might consider. One is with the company from which you purchase your machines and they offer a package of machines, location help, maybe even products. Then you buy everything from them and give them a percentage of your profit forever more. Another is what Coke and Pepsi offer. They will "give" you the machine, but you have to buy all of your drinks from them and you can't put any competitors' drinks in the machine. You also have to purchase a certain amount of product, as indicated by your contract, from them every month.

One of the best ways I have found to start your business is when you have enough financial capital to buy a route from someone (discussed further in Chapter 7). This gives you locations and machines, cutting out a lot of time and money. The cost of a route depends on the route size, machine worth, and the financial intake each machine on the route generates. The machines will be used, but as long as they work well, they will be fine. The locations need to be productive. You can determine that by checking the seller's financial intake per machine, per location. Having the machine bringing in an expected amount of money right from the start is less stressful. Less stress is a good thing.

The amount you pay for a route should be based on the amount of money you will be able to generate. In general, you pay 1½ years' worth of the route's gross income. The age of the machines will also be factored in. New machines that have not depreciated for their full seven years should be priced at the remaining depreciation value, so add that amount to the total of the route cost. Machines that are older than seven years should not cost you more than the location cost. If the seller isn't able to give you all of this information, or if the machines are dirty or empty, do not buy that route.

With less financial capital, you will need to grow slower. Perhaps you are still working. To grow slower, you will need to find locations first (see Chapter 7), then pay around $5,000 for new, $2,000 for refurbished, and $1,000 for used per machine. This way of doing things takes longer and is riskier because you never know beforehand if a location is going to generate the income you would like. Also, a new machine often has difficulties of its own with typical new machine kinks.

The advantage of building your business with new machines is locations often want them. Those new machines come with warranties and help lines to call for repairs. Buying a new machine for a location is fun because you have the newest toy to play with, but new machines are expensive. It will take a while for the cost of the machine to be covered by the money collected at the location. Granted, you can depreciate your assets on your taxes, so that takes some of the pain out of purchasing new.

I have used all of these approaches, except the franchise model, and find that buying routes are the most satisfactory way for me to build my business. Once I doubled my business with one route purchase. That was fun!

Also, I have purchased new, refurbished, and used machines and built the business one machine at a time. I determine the newness of machines based on what the location requires. If someone is selling a nice-looking used machine, I can put that almost anywhere. If the location requests a new machine, I decide what their usage will probably be, negotiate with them, and either give them a nice used or brand-new machine.

It is not financially responsible to buy a brand-new machine for a startup business that only has 10 employees. It's definitely worth placing a pristine model, however, at a new school where the kids are going to have access to the machines. If you have a warehouse location where the look of the machine doesn't matter, purchasing a well working used machine is perfectly acceptable.

CHAPTER 4

Drill Down in the Details

As you set the stage for business success, it is important to pay attention to some of the nitty-gritty organizational and promotional aspects of your business. This doesn't mean you can't change your mind after you get started, but it makes sense to think about these things, and why you want to do them in a certain way, before you dive in.

Fortunately, it is not difficult to understand how all this works. What you do want to pay attention to, though, is including the items we address in this chapter in your business plans. Entity decisions, branding, legal obligations, financial management, team decisions, and promotion are all critical areas to focus on as you're setting up your vending machine business. How you handle these decisions will affect how easy or difficult it is for you to build your company.

Business Structure

One of the decisions that a business owner has to make is the organizational structure of their business. There are four main types of business structures in the US: sole proprietorship, partnership, limited liability company and corporation. Each structure has different tax, income, and liability implications for business owners and their companies.

Sole proprietorship is the simplest organizational structure available for businesses. According to the Internal Revenue Service (IRS), it is the most common form of business in the US.[10] Businesses structured as a sole proprietorship allows the owner or owners to have total control over company operations. Businesses that typically form sole proprietorships are home-based businesses, shop or retail businesses, and one-person consulting firms. Owners of sole proprietor businesses are responsible for their own record keeping and paying the IRS in the form of self-employment taxes. That doesn't mean that you have to personally do this work. You can hire a bookkeeper and accountant, but the responsibility is all yours. The downside of this type of business is that it does not offer any liability protection for business owners; they can be held personally responsible for their company's debt and financial obligations as well as for liability issues.

A partnership is formed when two or more people join, or partner, together to run a business. Each partner has an equal share in the net profits and losses of their business. Like a sole proprietorship, each partner reposts their income on their personal tax return and pays self-employment taxes to the IRS. They are also personally liable for financial debt and obligations of their company and also the actions of other partners. Although partnerships can be formed through oral agreements and handshakes, written agreements are the best option in the event of disputes or lawsuits between partners.

The limited liability company (LLC) structure of business organization is considered a hybrid as they can be formed as corporations or partnerships. LLCs can provide owners, or members, the protection from liability and other obligations similar to a corporation. They can also be set up and managed like a partnership. The taxation of LLCs also depends on its structure.

Corporations are the most complex organizational structure for businesses. This type of business structure separates the liabilities and obligations that the company has from being the responsibility of the owners. Corporations are regulated by the laws of the state they are set up in. The IRS taxes corporation owners' salaries at individual tax rates. There are two common types of corporation structures: The difference between the two are the tax rules. Most corporations are C corporations; these are taxed as separate entities at corporate tax rates.

S corporations are pass-through entities meaning everything goes on the owners' personal tax returns. Both can pass income and losses onto their shareholders to avoid paying federal income taxes. This prevents double taxation of corporation profits.

You may find it valuable to invest in consulting with an attorney or CPA to ensure you are making the right structure choice for your business. Some people use Legal Zoom because they can help you with the structure and also offer help with insurance, business name searches, permit requirements, and taxes. Note, this is not considered legal advice. You should consult your own attorney or CPA for important matters that may have long-term consequences.

Business Name

Your business name plays a role in almost every aspect of your business, so you want it to be a good one. Make sure you think through all of the potential implications as you explore your options to choose your business name.

Once you have chosen a name for your business, you will need to check if it's trademarked or currently in use. Then, you will need to register it. A sole proprietor must register their business name with either their state or county clerk. Corporations, LLCs, or limited partnerships register their business name when the company formation paperwork is filed with the state.

Next, you'll need business cards made so you can hand them out and tape them to your machines. Don't overwhelm your cards with information. Your business name, your name, email address, and phone number are all that is necessary. Title, personal address and other details are all unnecessary. If you're looking for an inexpensive solution, Vistaprint often runs specials.

When I first started my business, I had an official name for tax purposes and had a DBA, "doing business as," name. The first iteration of my business was a C-corp, because I used my 403-B to help finance my startup. This way of financing meant that I had to have a corporate, third party, accounting company taking care of all of the corporation taxes and filings. I never put my official name on my business cards. Instead, I put my DBA on the card. My first DBA was Anne's Healthy Snacks. I thought that said it all because when I started, my plan was to offer only healthy snacks – wave of the future, right? Wrong.

Licenses and Permits

Paperwork is a part of the process when you start your own business. Registering your business with the state and federal governments is necessary. Unfortunately, we all have to pay taxes. Having a registered business will enable you to get a sales tax certificate that will also allow you to request a sales-tax-free designation from most suppliers. Registration for a tax identification number (TIN), also known as an Employer identification number (EIN), is free and easy on IRS.gov.

"An employer identification number (EIN) is a nine-digit number assigned by the IRS. It's used to identify the tax accounts of employers and other businesses who have no employees. The IRS uses the number to identify taxpayers who are required to file various business tax returns. This number is used instead of your social security number, so getting one also helps to protect your personal information. EINs are used by employers, sole proprietors, corporations, partnerships, non-profit associations, trusts, estates of decedents, government agencies, certain individuals, and other business entities.

The Internet is the preferred method to use when applying for an EIN. The online EIN application is available Monday-Friday, 7 a.m. to 10 p.m. Eastern time on IRS.gov. Once the application is completed and the information is validated during the online session, an EIN is issued immediately. Taxpayers who apply online can view, print, and save their EIN assignment notice at the end of the session (authorized third-party designees will receive the EIN; however, the EIN assignment notice will be mailed to the applicant). The online application isn't available for entities with foreign addresses."[11]

As far as tax filing is concerned, I recommend that you get a good accountant to walk you through all of the various forms and filings you will need to complete. Personally, I pay my sales and use tax quarterly, without the benefit of an accountant, because these tax filing requirements are fairly easy to understand. The first time I filed, I called the tax collector just to make sure I did everything correctly, but after one call I had it down pat.

Once I started paying myself, I hired ADP, a payroll processing company, to take care of all of those taxes and filings. Did you know that you have to pay unemployment tax even if you, the owner, are the only employee? It is crazy difficult for me to even imagine filing all of the employee and employer taxes. ADP is not the only business that helps with paying employees and taxes, they are just the one I used. CPAs and QuickBooks can also do this task. You will want to ask other small business owners who they use before committing to one company or individual.

My best advice for you regarding taxes is to keep all of your business expenses in an account totally separate from your personal expenses. You will want separate business and personal checking accounts, as well as credit cards. Also, keep track of your business mileage. Keeping business and personal accounts and spending separate will save a lot of time and grief when you have to file your taxes. It can also save you a lot of headaches if you're audited.

It's a good idea to have insurance for your assets. Some locations require that you provide proof of insurance. It will also come in handy if anyone decides to run over your machine or shake it so bad that it falls on them. Apparently, more people die by having vending machines fall on them than die by shark bite.

Accounting System

Small businesses run most effectively when there are systems in place. One of the most important systems for a small business is an accounting system. This is necessary in order to create and manage your budget, set your rates and prices, conduct business with others, and file your taxes. You can set up your accounting system yourself using a spreadsheet, buy a program to help you with accounting, or hire an accountant to take away some of the guesswork.

Your Team

If you will be hiring employees, now is the time to start the process. Make sure you take the time to outline the positions you need to fill and the job responsibilities that are part of each position. The Small Business Administration has an excellent guide to hiring your first employee that is useful for new small business owners.

If you are not hiring employees, but instead outsourcing work to independent contractors, now is the time to get your independent contractors lined up. One possible use for an independent contractor is to help you move machines occasionally, unless you have a truck with a lift gate and strong helpers. You might also want a contractor for repairs that you can't make on your own.

Lastly, if you are a true solopreneur hitting the small business road alone, you may not need employees or contractors, but you will still need your own support team. This team can be comprised of a mentor, small business coach, or even your family, and serves as your go-to resource for advice, motivation, and reassurance when the road gets bumpy.

Promote Your Small Business

Once your business is up and running, you need to start securing locations. You'll want to reference the marketing plan you wrote in your business plan. Then, explore as many small business marketing ideas as possible so you can decide how to promote your business most effectively. Other marketing venues include social media outlets and word-of-mouth from your current locations.

After having some challenges with the business, I found my SCORE mentor. Through working with him, I realized that my DBA needed to represent my actual business more than it did. I changed it to Healthy Vending Machines Raleigh Durham. That way, when people googled healthy vending, they would find my name and know that I serviced the Raleigh Durham area.

Well, healthy snacks are good in theory, but really everyone just wants junk food snacks. Since I wasn't making money just offering healthy snacks and was losing money on inventory as it expired because no one was eating it, I changed my DBA to Central Vending NC. I just felt guilty keeping the word healthy in the name since an average of 80% of my machines were filled with not so healthy stuff. With the word vending, people still saw me on Google, and with NC and Central, they knew what area I serviced. I had grown out of just Raleigh and Durham.

This leads nicely to the idea of having a website for your business. As you have probably gathered, I am not very good at making a website, so I hired someone else to do that fun chore. Your website can be very simple. On the home page you'll want to have your name, what you offer, and your story. Another page can have a contact form for people to fill out if they want you to give them a call. Be sure you know when your domain expires so you can renew it on time every year. Keep your website simple and be sure your designer connects messages from your contact page directly to your email.

Once you have completed these business start-up activities, you will have all of the most important bases covered. Keep in mind that success doesn't happen overnight. Use the plan you've created to consistently work on your business, and you will increase your chances of success.

CHAPTER 5

Choose the Right Vending Machine Equipment

Notice that I didn't say "purchase" the right vending machine; you need a location before you do that. There are many types of vending machines. The items you want to sell, the budget you have for your vending machine business, the location you are targeting, and the consumers you intend to have are all factors to consider when you decide to get into the vending machine business. Understanding how these issues relate to your objectives will help you find the best and most appropriate vending machine for your needs.

The Items You Want to Sell

To choose the right vending machine equipment you will need to decide what you want to sell. The vending machine equipment has to be able to vend what you want to sell and what your clients want to buy. Do you want to sell gumballs? You should buy a gumball machine. To sell snacks, you will need a snack machine, and for drinks you will need a drink machine.

Do you want to sell sandwiches? Your vending machine will have to be the type that can vend sandwiches in their different shapes and sizes and be refrigerated. Vending machines that sell soda, juice, bottled water, etc. will also need a cooling system. For frozen meals, ice cream, drumsticks, or other products that need to be kept frozen, you will want a vending machine freezer. In order to keep the compressor functioning properly in each of these machines (the freezer, drink and sandwich machines) and keep the products at the proper temperature, the machines need to be placed indoors. Nobody likes melted ice cream or a hot soda.

If you are starting with a budget on the smaller side (less than $500), there are smaller vending machines. These are called bulk candy machines and they contain candy, gumballs, chocolate, peanuts, and other small items. They are easier to maintain, cheaper, smaller in size, and lightweight. Some beginners in the vending machine industry favor the bulk candy machine to build their vending route. Some parents who want to encourage the entrepreneurial spirit in their kids will help them start a bulk vending business.

Some other bulk vending machines that are large in size are filled with candy, lollipops, gumballs, stickers, and small toys. Vending machines of this type may also offer games of chance with a crane activated on it so that when the users insert money, a claw will be activated to get items. From these vending machines, choose the type that you think is most appropriate for your intended business.

Once you decide what you want to sell (toys, electronics, gum, candy, chips, drinks), look at the size of the location and number of employees and customers to estimate usage and determine the size of the machine.

Buying Vending Machines

One way to find the machine you would like to use is to contact a vending machine distributor. Personally, I have used Wittern group, USI, Dixie Narco, and Crane. With them you have the option to choose from many different types of vending machines. Some distributors specialize in one type of vending machine, such as soda vending machines, whereas others have all kinds for you to choose from. Most of the distributors have a website where you can browse the list of used and new vending machines.

If you use a newer company, beware that their products have not been tested through time and may not hold up very well. In general, I would stick with a company that has been in business at least 10 years so they have a proven track record. I purchased my first five machines from a company that had been selling these machines for 1 year. The manufacturer went out of business the following year. Now I have trouble finding parts.

Take a look at the types and condition of the machines that a vending machine distributor has to sell. Most of the time you will see very little difference in a new and refurbished vending machine. The main difference will be in the price of each one; new costs the most and offers a guarantee, refurbished will cost less and usually offers a guarantee, and used vending machines cost the least but often don't come with any guarantee. Distributors of new vending machines also offer payment plans so that you can finance the cost of the machine over a period of time, saving you money on the initial investment. If you are not sure whether or not you will remain in the vending machine business, you can also lease the vending machines from bulk vending distributors.

Coke and Pepsi have a program where they will give you a new machine. To join this program, contact your local Coke or Pepsi distributor, and fill out the information requested. If the company accepts you into their program, they will have you sign a contract stating that you will purchase a certain number of pallets of drinks from them on a certain schedule. The company will then deliver the agreed upon products to your storage facility at the agreed upon time interval. As long as you honor the contract, the company will supply you with a new machine and will repair it as needed.

You can easily find a vending machine distributor by searching online. Distributors of vending machines often will deliver the machines to you. Most, but not all, will also arrange to pick them up if you decide you no longer want to use the machines, or you want to get out of the business.

Delivery and pick up services are not the same with all distributors. Before purchasing a machine find out exactly what their policies are for delivery and pick up. Will they place and balance the machine at your location for you? Or are they going to leave the machine in your driveway for you to unwrap, test, and move to your location? Will they send out a repair person if the machine doesn't work properly? Or will you have to call the company to walk you through repairs, which is also a good option since you will learn how to repair the machine using this method. What is the return policy for picking up your machine if you have any problems?

There are also bulk vending distributors that sell vendable products only and do not deal in the vending machines themselves. They have a wide variety of supplies that you can purchase for stocking your vending machines. If you decide on the bulk vending business, you can get a good estimate of the costs involved in operating the business by visiting bulk vending sites and warehouse sites. Bulk vending distributors do not take back any supplies that you purchase, and you have to purchase everything in bulk. However, you may be able to sell what you have left over to another person just getting started in the vending machine business as long as the products have not passed their use by date.

Distributors of vending machines deal directly with the manufacturers and they also have great associations with other vending business owners. If you want to find a vending route for sale, one source of information is a vending machine distributor. In dealing with the various operators, the distributor will be able to tell you why the person is selling the route and whether or not they think it would be profitable for you to buy it. Used machines and routes can potentially be found in several locations. You can look for advertisements on Facebook Marketplace, OfferUp, eBay, LetGo, Craigs List, and vending machine warehouses in the area.

Some questions to ask when looking to buy a refurbished, used, or new vending machine include:

- How much space will the machine take up at a location? Each location will have a certain amount of space that they allow for a vending machine. You want to make sure that your machine isn't too big for that space.

- Will the machine be easy to maintain? Different machines have different levels of difficulty when it comes to maintenance and technology. You need to know how to clean, price, and test everything. You'll also need to learn how to empty the coin mechanism and bill validator.

- Does the machine vend a variety of snacks and drinks with different size containers? If it does, you need to know if you can order different parts to accommodate these different sizes and shapes.

- Are parts easy to buy for the machine if you decide you want to vend an item that is an unusual size or shape?

- Will help be easily available for programming the machine? They should be able to give you a number or person to call when your machine isn't working. This is also a good way to find vending machine repair people.

- Does the machine have a warranty if anything should break down?

- Do all of the parts work – coils, coin mechanism, dollar valida-tor, card reader?
- Is the machine credit card able?
- Is the compressor working?
- Does it look good enough for the location you're taking it to?
- When the machine is shipped to your location, will the shippers unwrap and set up the machine?

A common misconception about choosing the vending machine type is that newer is better. New machines are nice because they come with warranties and technical assistance as needed. New machines might also look prettier, but if you buy a used machine that doesn't have as many computerized parts, they have fewer problems. If you purchase a used machine with all of the computerized parts, the former owner would have worked out all of the kinks. Another option for purchasing a machine is a refurbished machine. These often come with warranties and the company that you purchase these machines from provides technical support. Refurbished costs less than new but more than used.

I thought my brand spanking new machines would be the best choice when I first started. Boy, was I wrong! I have replaced every computer board on all of those machines as well as most of the motors and compressors. On the other hand, I bought some used machines from a reputable dealer and have never had any problems.

The most common problem I have heard about when it comes to using the incorrect vending machine for the product it was designed for is jamming, either in the coils or at the product bin door. One person I know had a refrigerated machine that had wide coils, so he decided to sell sandwiches and soups. The problem occurred when the customer tried to get the item out of the product bin door, the product wouldn't come out, they had to mutilate the item to get it out of the door.

Another example of having the incorrect machine was when one of my clients had several employees that went on the Keto diet and they wanted Keto snacks. Nuts worked great, but then I tried to vend beef jerky and the sticks kept getting caught up in the coils and wouldn't vend. I had to switch that out for Mama's Hot Sausage because they were thick enough to vend properly. Thankfully, they went off that diet fad fairly quickly.

My recommended process is to find out exactly what the client wants from their vending machine and purchase the machine that fulfills their needs.

The Location You Are Targeting

A good question to ask potential locations before you purchase a machine for them is "Why do you want vending machines at your business?" Having an idea of why they are offering machines helps you know what kinds of foods and drinks to offer.

Do they want to offer affordable, easy snacks at their hotel, or do they want their guests to be able to grab a drink while they wait for service at their auto shop? What space is available and is there room for more than one machine? Some locations can handle both a snack and drink machine, while others may need a smaller combo unit.

Lastly, what are the demographics of the location? Is there a predominance of younger people who may prefer high energy drinks or an older clientele that might like soft snacks that are easy to chew. Are there more men or women? Locations that have a higher proportion of women than men sell more chocolate products so you will want more varieties available in the machine. More men at a location will require more chips and breakfast items. Making sure you have the right product mix in your machine, which means providing the customer with what they most want to buy, is important if you want the location to be profitable.

The business locations you chose will have a lot to do with the machines and products you choose to keep in stock. For example, if you want to focus on a health club or gym, you may have a vending machine offering sports drinks, water and healthy snacks. If you want to focus on school campuses, you might want a machine that sells candy bars, chips and cookies.

One of my locations wanted all types of drinks that come in different shapes and sizes. Red Bull was something they requested. This only vends in a Red Bull vending machine unless you have a vending machine that doesn't use the stack and rotate system that is common in most drink machines or have a machine that offers shims for smaller items. Luckily, I had a drink machine available that could vend various shapes and sizes of drinks.

The Customers You Intend to Have

Another aspect of the vending machine that you should consider, especially if you're purchasing a used machine, is whether or not it is credit card enabled (MDB compatible). Some locations don't want credit card readers (why, I don't know), but more are starting to request them. New machines all come credit card enabled, but some of the older ones do not.

When deciding on the credit card readers and remote monitoring, you should look at all of the available companies and decide which one will work best for you. There are several companies that make credit card readers. The charges to you include a monthly fee and a percentage of your sales. Each company has a different cost for these fees and services. I personally use USA Vend Tech and Cantaloupe; however, there are others that may fit your needs better, such as Nayax.

The way to set up a credit card account on your machine is to fill out a contract with the credit card company that includes your business bank account information. The credit card company will send you the money your customers spent using a credit card on purchases directly into your account, usually on a weekly basis. The company will take the money you owe them out of the total amount the customer spent. The break down for these fees can be found on the credit card company's website or by calling the company.

Something to keep in mind when deciding if you want to offer credit card readers is that annual cashless sales have increased by close to 40% each year up through 2019. Also, the average cash transaction was $22, and the average non-cash transaction was $112 in 2019.[12]

Lastly, always use a good surge protector on your machines. Energy surges can ruin your motherboard and mess with all of your settings.

CHAPTER 6

Locate Machines - It Really is All About Location!

The vending business is attractive to entrepreneurs because it creates a mostly passive income. There are nearly 5 million vending machines in the United States right now, generating over $7 billion in total annual sales and $64 million a year in profit for the snack niche alone.[13]

However, it takes work to get those vending machines generating income while you sleep. The next step toward creating a profitable vending business, after defining your goals and deciding what you want to vend, is to choose the right location. A vending machine that no one sees cannot generate any revenue.

Profitable vending machine locations are plentiful, but identifying them and securing them can take some work. The vending business can generate significant passive income once you put in the upfront work to secure great locations. Make sure you're continually scouting for new locations and building connections in your community to open new possibilities for revenue and profits.

You might think you could place a vending machine anywhere, but that's not reality. First, you cannot legally place a machine on someone else's property and use their utilities without their permission or a contract. Second, not every location is ideal for a vending machine. What good is a vending machine that sits idle with no passersby? When starting or expanding a vending business, it is important to find the most profitable potential locations.

In the vending business, as in the real estate market, success is all about location, location, location. A profitable business begins with choosing the right locations, which involves some research and some visits to the prospective location to evaluate traffic, study your competition, and secure permission from property owners. A business office on the top floor of a building with 20 people who go out to lunch at the café next door is not a good choice.

Without people, you cannot have a profitable vending business. Foot traffic is the key ingredient to a successful vending machine. Vending purchases often fall into one of two categories – impulse buys or habitual buys. People either grab something when they are in need of a quick pick-me-up or a snack catches their eye, or they get in the habit of making a purchase from a machine they see every day in their break room at work, their school, or in their apartment or condominium building.

When it comes to foot traffic, you want to find locations where a large number of people walk by every single day like shopping centers, schools, gyms, etc. For places like offices, you usually need a minimum of 50 full-time employees to generate sufficient revenue for profits.

Every area where people work, attend school, or make things need vending machines. The prospecting aspect of the business was the most difficult for me. I don't like to sell things to people. I'm uncomfortable meeting people for the first time when I'm asking them for something. I had to change my thought process so that I would see prospecting as me offering them something for free. I'm offering to put one of my vending machines in their business for their customers' and employees' convenience. Finding new locations is a very important aspect of this business. You won't have a business if you don't have customers.

Prospect – Find the Location

Now that you have decided what type of product you would like to sell, and the type of machine you will use, you are ready to network into your ideal location.

The vending machine business, like any other, is meant to make a profit. The location is a very important aspect of ensuring your business is sustainable. Even with the right research, there's no guarantee for a good profit, but you can stack the odds in your favor by looking for the following:

- Areas with high foot traffic such as malls and entertainment venues, or residential complexes
- Large offices or multi-business office parks, manufacturing plants, schools and universities with at least a few hundred people going there daily
- Locations with few or no other food and beverage options such as parks, jails, motels, gas stations, and service businesses
- Places that require a lot of waiting such as car repair shops, airports, bus and train stations, hospitals, medical centers, and salons. Even a public library is a good location from that perspective

When deciding whether to put a particular vending machine in a location or not, consider not only the surrounding area, but also who the target customer is. Different products work better with different demographics – child-friendly snacks along with gumballs or candies with pictures of soccer players or cartoon characters work best near schools. Healthy snacks, protein bars, and dried fruit are a good choice of selection if your vending machine is located in front of a gym.

When looking for great, profitable locations for your vending machines, you can approach new businesses in the area as well as existing ones. When it comes to businesses moving into an area, the first vending machine business that gets to them with a reasonable proposal may win out over the others. If you want that to be you, it makes sense to pay attention to the commercial ebb and flow of companies in your area. Business journals and online announcements may help keep you informed so you can offer to fulfill their vending needs before other providers contact them. In smaller towns and rural areas, local newspapers may offer more information. Joining local business organizations is another great way to not only keep abreast of any development or influx of new companies into the area, but also to network with existing business owners and get their referrals as well.

Gather research on existing companies that may need vending machines. As you travel around to different businesses in your area, take notes about the basic things that make a place a good or bad location for your vending machines. For example, when you go to get your car serviced, check out the vending options available.

You can also ask existing businesses for a chance to place your vending machines with them. Unless it is a brand-new building, the premises will probably already have vending machines operated by one of your competitors, but you shouldn't miss the opportunity to place a machine anyway. Even if vending machines are already installed in the location, see if you have something different to offer that the owner may prefer. Placing your machines in such locations can be highly profitable.

Talk to the property manager or business owner and ask if they are happy with their current vender; sometimes they are not and just haven't thought to find someone new. Pay attention to what they tell you. There might be some key information for you in reading between the lines. After the business has given notice to the current vending machine operator and that person has removed their machine, you can place your machines.

It is possible that the business owner does not have a positive relationship with the current vending machine business owner, or they are dissatisfied with the service. Old, dirty, damaged, or poorly maintained and stocked machines, machines with poor selection or selection different from yours, machines that operate only with cash – all these signs give you the perfect opportunity to approach the management with a better alternative. And even when you do not notice these signs, remember, every single business is run by people. Their reasons for switching vending machine services might be something one cannot see.

Just what are some of the best locations for vending machines? Every site a vending operator considers should be evaluated individually, but these are ten of the most ideal locations to pursue as far as my research for this book is concerned.

Restaurants

Restaurants are a great location for vending machines. Anyone who has ever worked in a restaurant knows that shifts are long, and breaks are nearly impossible to guarantee. Vending machines in employee break rooms give restaurant staff a way to stay energized and full during working hours.

Apartment Complexes

Apartment complexes are filled with active people constantly coming and going 24 hours a day, seven days a week. Many complexes also have laundry rooms, common areas, playgrounds and parks, party rooms, or gyms. These are great locations for vending machines since all members of the community have access to those spaces and many residents utilize those areas on a regular basis. One or more locations on the property can be ideal spots to place vending machines with a wide selection of food and beverage products.

Boys and Girls Clubs

Boys and Girls Clubs give children safe places to go after school where they are supervised by mentors who help them with their homework, organize games and activities, as well as with life skills and more. And what does every child want and need after school? A snack. However, because Boys and Girls Clubs and similar community organizations are about helping children reach their potential, junk food vending machines are not great choices. These organizations are a good location for healthy vending machines to give children better options for after-school snacks. This is especially true when you consider many of those same children come from food-insecure homes and they may not eat much, if at all, until they go back to school in the morning.

Hotels and Motels

Hotel and motel guests are captive audiences. Even if a hotel has a restaurant, not every guest wants a full meal or wants to pay for a full meal. Some hotels have micro-markets, but those are typically in the lobby and not every guest wants to make the trip to the lobby for a quick snack – especially if they can grab one on their floor. Placing vending machines in the lobby, side entrances, and ice machine areas can be a great way to generate continuous revenue.

Gyms

People who go to gyms work up an appetite. Post-workout they don't necessarily want to stop at the drive-through next door. They want something healthy. Gyms and fitness centers are ideal locations for vending machines that offer healthy snacks and drinks that can help people refuel after working up a sweat. The employees who work there also appreciate a vending machine with healthy options, since they are typically hourly workers who only receive short breaks. In one of my vending machines located at a gym I also offer socks because people often forget socks when packing in the morning for the gym after work.

Offices

Businesses with fifty or more employees are great locations for vending machines. Employees get hungry and thirsty throughout the day. Vending machines provide options for people who don't pack drinks, snacks, or lunches for themselves, which in today's busy world, includes most people.

Similarly, manufacturing facilities and industrial parks are great locations for vending machines. These businesses employ hundreds of people (typically 24 hours a day) who get short breaks but need to stay on their toes. Placing vending machines in the break room gives them options and provides the vending business with a great source of steady income.

Supermarkets and Retail Stores

In a supermarket or retail store, there are two specific audiences for vending machines. First, the customers coming in and out of the store. People often get hungry and thirsty while they are running errands. A vending machine placed near an entrance can be a great way to capture foot traffic and leverage impulse buys.

The second audience includes the employees. Retail employees usually get one or two ten-minute breaks a shift and a short meal break. They usually don't have time to run to a restaurant to grab a meal or snack. Vending machines provide an affordable opportunity to fuel up before returning to work.

Laundromats

It can take someone anywhere from one hour to four hours to do their laundry in a laundromat. If you look, you'll see people doing homework or work, reading books, watching movies, or playing games to pass the time. Those people also get hungry and thirsty while they wait for the laundry to finish. Vending machines with a selection of beverages and snacks ensure customers don't have to abandon their laundry in search of food or drink. Laundromats are also a great place to cultivate repeat business, since most customers do their laundry at the same location at the same time, each week. Vending machines can become a natural part of their weekly routine.

Schools, Community Colleges and Universities

Students are busy and have healthy appetites. Schools, community colleges and universities are filled with activity and active people every day. Vending machines in the right locations on a school property can be an excellent source of revenue as hundreds of people pass by every day. Elementary, Middle and High schools are particularly ideal for vending machines that sell healthy products because parents and administrators want to ensure students have access to better options than chips, cupcakes, and sodas during the day. Community College and University students will want and expect the standard vending machine food, none of that healthy stuff.

College dorms are also excellent spots for vending machines. Students stay up late. They don't always want to run out for a snack while they are up working or hanging out with their friends. It's easy to go to a vending machine, especially if the machine can be programmed to take bank cards, credit cards, or even school meal plan cards.

When offering to vend for a school, there are considerations that should be taken into account. One is that you usually have to bid for the school contract. In that bid you should include your proof of liability insurance.

Find out beforehand how much liability insurance the school system requires; usually it's between $1 and $2 million. This insurance will cost less than $1,000 per year. Also, be up to date on the USDA smart snack guidelines for the Elementary, Middle, and High Schools.

Shopping Centers and Malls

Vending machines provide mall shoppers with a fast, convenient, and more affordable option for a snack or beverage than the food court. Machines placed at entrances, exits, and strategic locations throughout the center gives those shoppers a way to grab something quick without standing in line or waiting for meal prep. Try to have healthy options in all of your vending machines. Healthy options in shopping centers work well because many parents would rather give their kids something healthy to munch on to keep them content. This avoids the sugar high that all parents dread.

Malls are also a great place to get creative with your placement. Abandoned storefronts that are generating no revenue for the mall can be a smart place to position your vending machines. If the shopping center has requested, and you have given a percentage of your profits, this will help the shopping center generate some revenue out of the empty store and gives shoppers a reason to keep walking past the abandoned store to other areas of the mall.

Always be ready to market your vending machine business and yourself. You should be prepared to approach a location owner and ask to talk with him about the opportunities you can offer. Even if you are just starting out, it is important to present yourself as a successful business owner. You are not just a person off the street begging property owners to let you put a machine in their building. You are a business owner with a mutually beneficial offer. Perhaps you even have an excellent logo design, attractive company uniforms, and professional literature, which will help them take you more seriously.

Vending locations don't always go the way you might think. Consider the following surprising real-life stories about my experiences with an automobile show room, an office building, a car repair garage, and a bank.

The automobile showroom wanted to switch to their corporation's machines. The location was a fairly good one, but not great. You might think this would be a good location because it had a waiting room for the people having their cars serviced, and you are right about that. However, it was also not such a good location because they offered free coffee, tea and water, as well as cookies and donuts to those customers. People usually don't want to pay for something when they can get something similar for free. Some people wanted candy and soda, so the machines did make some money, but they would have made a lot more without the competition.

Another location I had that should have been fairly good was an office building. They had 40 employees and no other food options around. I was so excited to have a machine in their break room. The problem was that on move-in day they asked me to put my machine in a locked closet outside of the break room. I couldn't believe it. The administrative assistant told me that she would send out an email to all of the employees telling them about the machine. She also told me that everyone had a pass card that would let them into the closet to get snacks when they wanted them. I kept my machine at their location for a couple months because I thought that, in time, people would realize the machine was there and start to use it. That never came to be. I made about $10 per week at that location. With such dismal profits, it was easy to find a better location.

At one point, I purchased a route from a man who didn't keep his machines very clean. I thought that was OK because I could easily clean them, and the clean machines would bring in more money. For the most part that was true, but one of his machines was kept in the back room of a repair garage. No one used the machine because it was difficult to reach. I even had to climb over boxes to get to it. I quickly found a better location and moved that machine out.

I think the worst location I've had was a bank. The physical location should have been good since it was in the lobby of a four-story bank with over 50 employees. The problem was one very unhappy person and one very young building operations guy. The unhappy person always complained about everything, including the vending machine. The operations guy wanted to keep everyone in the building happy. I was called every week about something being wrong. Once this unhappy person lost a nickel in the machine. How that was possible I still don't know. Another time she received a bag of chips that didn't have as many chips as she thought there should be. Then she complained that I didn't get her nickel to her fast enough. Granted, it took two days for me to find time to return to the location, but still, it was a nickel. Thank goodness I was scheduled to visit the location the day after she was given the bad bag of chips and was able to replace it quickly. After a month the very young building operator asked me to take the machines out because he was getting too many complaints. I always wondered why they had asked the previous vending machine operator to move out. Now I know.

CHAPTER 7

Secure Locations

How does a person secure a high-quality vending machine location? By generating high quality leads. To generate high quality leads you need to research the market area. One way to research is to ask the chamber of commerce in your town for a list of businesses with 50 or more employees. That is what I did first. I obtained a list of all of the businesses in my area that had 50 or more employees and called each one asking if they needed a vending machine. I called around 25 businesses and two of them became customers. So, you can decide if you want to go that route.

Another way to obtain leads is to network within the business community. I joined five networking groups through recommendations from other small business owners and attended their meetings. By doing this, joining the five groups, I found six locations.

Next I learned about buying someone else's route. A woman in my city saw my business card on one of my machines and called me to find out if I would be interested in buying her route. That includes the machines and locations.

Another way to find a lead, or prospect, is to use a vending machine locator service to do the research for you. While it may seem easier to hire a locator service to find the best places for your vending machines, they do not have the best reputation when it comes to looking out for your bottom line. They usually also charge large fees. They may even require a considerable percentage of their fee upfront for finding a location. This practice opens the doors for scammers who charge a fee but never actually find a location for you. Unscrupulous location finders can also convince you to put a machine at a certain location they have not researched appropriately. As long as they have their money, they could find any location they want without doing the research to ensure that site will be profitable for you.

One of the main reasons why vending machine locator services often fail to deliver on their promises is that their people are incentivized in ways that work against your best interests. All they have to do is find a location owner or manager who is willing to accommodate a vending machine to collect a fee from you. They have absolutely no responsibility or guarantees to ensure your products will sell in that location. And, you, as a vending machine owner, have no data to go on until the machine sits there for several months so you can gather information on sales, profits, and expenses.

If you wish to avoid all these problems with a locator service, you must take special care to find a reputable one. They can be very helpful if you do not have the time or ability to identify the best locations for your vending machines on your own, provided you engage the right one.

One of the best ways to find a quality vending machine locator service is to ask other people in the industry which ones they have used successfully in the past. Honest reviews and testimonials can help you decide. The company should be willing to put a contract in writing and clearly outline everything they are responsible for along with all of the tasks they will complete. If you do not understand any part of the contract, they should be willing to go over it with you or allow you to take it to a lawyer. Some information that should be covered includes all fees and commission payments if any, terms of payment and legal relationship, and basic information such as the general area you are interested in, the number of vending machines you want to place, the type of products you offer, and your preferred customers.

If you do not have the funds to hire a location service or want to have a more hands-on approach with your vending machine business, you can go out and find great locations on your own. Since the success or failure of your business is your responsibility and a large part of your business relies on the locations of your machines, taking care of this part on your own instead of hiring a service makes sound business sense.

Qualifying Leads

Converting leads and optimizing the initial business is very important to the financial success of your business. To do this, you need to learn what the estimated foot traffic of the location is likely to be along with the number of employees. A total of more than 50 people potentially using the machine is ideal. You also need to look at the location where they want the machine placed. If it's a closet, don't take it!!! The best machine location is in the breakroom or cafeteria.

Find out if there are other food services available close by and what they are. My best locations by far are companies in the middle of nowhere. They can't run out to McDonalds for a burger during their half hour break. My least productive locations are the offices that are right in the middle of areas with several very good food options. If there is a gas station next door, your drink sales won't be as good as if that gas station is over a mile away.

It's important to ask the prospective location about what type of vending they require and what problems they think having that vending machine will solve. You have to decide if you want to vend those items or negotiate them away. I had a location that wanted sandwiches, but I didn't have the money for a new machine, or the desire to vend sandwiches. I asked, instead, if I could still put my drink and snack machines in their location. They said yes because they couldn't find anyone who would vend sandwiches. I stayed at that location for 8 wonderful years, until they found a sandwich vendor and I had to leave.

Set up an appointment to talk with the property owner or manager of a location in which you wish to place a vending machine. Be pleasant, positive, and professional from the first handshake, present your business card, and smile at the end of the meeting while you thank him for his time and promise to follow up. Expect the meeting to be quick. Prepare ahead of time so that all important information is shared. List the benefits of properly maintained and stocked vending machines such as employee satisfaction, increased foot traffic, and more patient customers at a service business.

If you have identified a location that has existing vending machines on site already, you should ask the owner if he is satisfied with the relationship. If they answer "No," you have the perfect opportunity to offer something better. If they answer "Yes," it is important to follow up with the unique benefits that your vending machine business can offer. This could be a different type of product, exceptionally better service, or a personal touch that only you can provide. The most important thing is to make the location owner feel vital and appreciated throughout the entire process. Even if the property owner decides he does not want your vending machines at his location, always leave with a smile, a handshake, and a 'thank you' for his time. Leave a business card and ask him to keep you in mind if anything changes.

Record all the locations visited, owners or managers and their responses by date.

While a business owner or property manager may say "No" to you once, that does not have to be the final answer for all time. You should, of course, never harass or continuously bug someone to try to get their business. However, you can make a follow-up contact after a few months or a year to keep your vending machine business fresh in their mind.

Contacts in the future may come at the perfect moment when the vending company they were using pulls out or fails to satisfy their vending needs. You should always be ready and willing to provide top-quality service and products the moment they change their mind.

If the location does want one of your machines placed at their location, you will want a signed contract in order to place your machines. In some cases, it will be very easy to land a contract and in other cases, you'll have to jump through quite a few hoops. In some situations, business owners will want a percentage of the profits from your machines to offset the cost of their utilities and generate some passive income of their own. I try to avoid contracts like these because I am providing them with a service, and I am a small business. However, if they have to have a percentage, I increase the product cost by that percentage to make up for the loss of income. When locations get a commission for machine placement, it's 5-10% in my area, but this can vary a lot across the country. Businesses want to keep their employees and clients happy with reasonably priced snacks, so most locations don't even ask for a percentage.

Take time before and after the location meeting to establish a level of trust and personal connection. Usually, by the time locations reach the meeting point, they want your business. Always leave your meeting with the people smiling. Prepare and sign a contract either before the meeting ends or within five business days of getting an agreement.

Once you have your vending machine placed, remember it is vital to get the best location within the right location. A vending machine stuck in the back corner won't bring you the expected financial results. Try to get it located at the front counter or near the front door.

Below is an example of a vending contract. I am not an attorney and this sample contract is in no way legal advice. Be sure to have any legal document you sign vetted by a lawyer you trust.

FULL-SERVICE VENDING AGREEMENT

This agreement made this **20ᵗʰ** day of **Jan 20xx** by and between **Vending – Phone: (123) 451-7890** - hereafter referred to as **VENDOR** and – **Company,** Inc - hereafter referred to as LOCATION. In consideration of the mutual covenants herein, the parties do agree as follows:

LOCATION grants to VENDOR the exclusive rights and privilege to sell and dispense snacks, cold beverages, and any other products contained in the vending proposal (as may be modified either orally or in writing, from time to time, by mutual Agreement of the parties) at its LOCATION. LOCATION grants VENDOR access during all business hours to the LOCATION's premises for the purposes of providing service and maintenance.

VENDOR is acknowledged to be the owner of all machines, equipment and/or merchandise which may be brought upon LOCATION's property by VENDOR and nothing in the Agreement will give LOCATION any interest in such machines, equipment and/or merchandise. Any damage done to machines or liability from the machines will be covered by VENDOR's insurance. If there is a major equipment failure, VENDOR will make every effort to complete repair within twenty-four hours of receipt of parts necessary to make the repair. Refilling service will be provided by VENDOR on an "as needed" basis and VENDOR will make every effort to respond to LOCATION's calls within two (2) business days.

CANCELLATION WITHOUT CAUSE - Either party may provide written notice of cancellation to the other party at least thirty days before the expiration of the original term or any renewal term.

CANCELLATION WITH CAUSE - Additionally, should either party feel that the other has failed to observe all the covenants contained herein, it shall notify the other party of its breach in writing.

If within ten (10) days of the notice the breach has not been corrected, then the other party may cancel the agreement. Any single vending machine with over two-thirds of its selections empty for a period exceeding 7 days will be considered an automatic breach of this agreement and will waive the LOCATION's requirement to provide a "10-day notice to correct" as mentioned above.

This document constitutes the entire agreement of the parties. **The parties and their assignees are bound by this agreement**.

LOCATION and VENDOR, having read and agreed to all the terms herein, have signed the Agreement.

DATE: 20Jan20xx   Signatures:

This agreement is included within the toolkit of ideas and forms which is offered as a special bonus; you can claim it for free here:

https://www.VendingBusinessBook.com/gift

CHAPTER 8

Source the Best-Selling Vending Machine Products at the Best Price

Who are your customers and what do they want? Every location is unique in demographics, traffic, and requirements so products should be customized to the location. Something I have always found fascinating are the differences in snack choice from location to location. An all-male, blue collar location almost always wants Pepsi products and pastry breakfast items. An all-female health center wants lots of chocolate. Assisted living locations eat more candy than chips. Whereas a younger person's location eats more chips. Almost all of my locations want Peanut M&M's.

When deciding what to stock in your machine, consider the location. Consider what the people at the location want in their machine. Schools usually have snack and drink requirements that are strict: 50% whole grain, less than 200 calories. Nutritional value is important to some locations. Some companies want healthy snacks for insurance purposes. Healthy items are getting easier to find in the warehouse stores. However, in general, the healthier the item, the more expensive.

Which brings us to other considerations such as the product taste. If you don't like it, what are the chances that others will? Affordability is another issue. If the products are too expensive, no one will purchase them. Brand recognition is important. People don't usually like to try things they have never tried before, so it is a good idea to stick with brands that are common when you first enter a location. You can try the novelty items after you are more established and can give out samples of the new items.

Sourcing

Source options for your snacks and drinks include wholesaler sources, such as United Natural Foods Inc, and Vistar, if you have good storage and lots of machines so you can handle the pallets they deliver. There are also cash and carry suppliers, and brokers of specialty products. Membership clubs like Costco are another option. They have more of the healthy choices available. Sam's has more of the vending food and drink that is typically found in vending machines. BJ's doesn't have the greatest selection but are worth checking out. And last, but not least, grocery stores, which often run good drink promotions.

Wholesaler Sources

Pros: Wholesalers usually offer the widest selection of product types at the lowest prices available. Some wholesalers have more than 1000 or even up to 50,000 different individual items to choose from. You can find regular sized and king-sized products, and everything from bubblegum to sunflower seeds, potato chips, candy, and beverages. Wholesalers supply anything you can imagine selling in your vending machine.

Besides having extensive lists of items to choose from, wholesalers are frequently better positioned to quickly distribute products to you. A vending machine business owner sometimes needs replacement product in a hurry, so a wholesale distribution center that can ship within 24 or 48 hours can be great to have on your side. While it is possible to drive to local wholesale centers, having product shipped saves you a lot of time.

Cons: As convenient as shipping is, sending large quantities of product can become quite expensive. Additional fees may be charged if you order a smaller number of products than their usual load. All of these extra payments must be added into your overhead and used when figuring out how much each individual unit costs. Shipping fees can cut into your profits considerably.

For smaller vending machine businesses with less than a dozen machines, a wholesale supplier's bulk sizes may be too large for you to use before their sell by date. While the products can be cheaper at the start, there will be more waste if things do not sell as quickly as you had hoped. More waste equals lower profits.

Cash & Carry Suppliers

Pros: Cash and carry suppliers are usually associated with a particular wholesale distributor, such as Vistar, one of the largest, who runs Merchant's Mart. These supply companies or departments offer case lots of popular products that your vending machine business can order and then pick up at any one of their locations. They also cater to small mom-and-pop stores and other vendors.

Two of the main benefits of cash and carry suppliers is the number of products available and the convenience. Since they are usually attached to a larger wholesale dealer, they carry the same product lines in smaller quantities. Also, the day you order is frequently the day you pick up your cases. Then you can drive off to service vending machines right away.

Most of the cash and carry suppliers who work with vending companies do not have premium membership requirements, so there are no extra fees associated with your wholesale purchase.

Even though these places are called cash and carry distributors, many accept major credit cards as well.

Cons: Some of the conveniences of cash and carry suppliers can also work against them. For example, if you live or work far away from the physical location, drive time and gas costs can eat into your profits. There are also some instances when the products offered in these smaller quantities have a slight increase in price per unit. This is simply because more packaging time and material and manpower go into creating the caseloads as opposed to leaving products in their original pallets. Since it is more beneficial for the wholesale suppliers to sell in large quantities to more active vending machine businesses, selling directly to small startups is not always in their best interest. Because more work is involved, they raise prices accordingly.

Brokers of Specialty Products

Pros: Vending machine business brokers who specialize in particular product lines are like freelance agents who research areas and demographic information and provide recommendations for hot products and where to get them. They usually work with more than one vending company and may be used by your competitors as well as your own company. Brokers not only give information and share resources, but they can also purchase wholesale products for you to sell. They negotiate with manufacturers to get special bulk discounts or rebates on larger quantities that isn't available to your individual company. These savings are shared with you and other vending machine businesses. This lowers your initial costs and improves profits.

Although it does cost money to use one of these vending machine business brokers, they can be quite valuable. This is especially true for beginners who do not understand or have the manpower to track sales trends and analyze profits over time in order to pick the best products or routes. The terms on how you'll be billed for the service will be negotiated in a contract. Some ways these brokers are paid can be by percentage of sales, a month-to-month consulting fee, or an annual consulting fee.

Cons: The majority of specialty brokers work primarily with large and established vending machine businesses with bigger budgets and more work to pass along. There may be "boutique" brokers who focus on particular niches or market their services to startups, but this is usually less profitable for them, so it is a rare situation. If you do hire a broker at the start of your vending machine business, you will undoubtedly be assigned a junior broker who is still learning. This can mean fewer contacts and less skill at tracking trends.

Many brokers are associated with a particular brand name of food, beverages and other products. Their goal is to sell as much product from that company as possible and not necessarily improve your vending business or increase your profitability. They may be able to get you discount prices on bulk goods, but you will need to pay close attention to how much you can actually use in order to prevent waste. If you do go with a broker of specialty goods for your vending machine business, find out who they represent and if they are paid on a commission. Brokers who are paid on commission will be less likely to have your best interests at heart.

Membership Clubs

Membership clubs are very popular in the United States. There is probably one or more of them conveniently located just a short drive away from wherever you do business. You can even find one along your vending route so you can make a quick stop to restock on popular products. This cuts down on both time and travel costs.

Pros: Costco, Sam's Club, and BJ's are all examples of membership clubs from which vending machine businesses can buy products. Although they are open to members of the public who purchased a membership, these clubs are also attractive sources for wholesale products intended for vending machine resale. In that way, they are very similar to cash and carry suppliers. As long as you live or work nearby, these stores are very convenient for buying anything from candy to soda to pretzels. The situation is perfect if you have a vending machine that sells out more quickly than you expected and your wholesale shipment is not due for several days. You can just run to the membership club and buy everything you need to restock.

When it comes to cost, membership clubs do not put a considerable markup on the wholesale prices they get. Since they are such large companies themselves, they can buy in massive bulk quantities at special discount prices from the manufacturers themselves. These initial savings are then passed on to you.

Quantities are high and costs are low. Most memberships clubs allow you to return unused products for a full refund. Wholesalers, on the other hand, may charge return and restocking fees.

Cons: It is necessary to pay an annual fee to gain access to these membership clubs, but it is usually less than $100 per year. The main problem with using membership clubs as a supplier in your vending machine business is that their selection of vending products may be low, and they may not always carry the same brands each time you go. There also may be limited sizes or flavors available for the different products and preferences. For example, Sam's Club sells primarily smaller sized beverages instead of 20-ounce bottles. If your vending strategy focuses on a vast selection of unique products, you may have to augment your membership club purchases with cash and carry or wholesale sources as well.

The size of your vending machine business may determine the source of your products. Your vending machine business can use any one of these product suppliers or try a combination for different reasons. The main determination may come down to size. If you operate a well-established vending business with dozens of machines, a wholesale or product broker may work best for you. If you have less than a dozen vending machines and are just starting out, membership clubs and cash and carry shops may help you afford varied inventory without taking on excess risk while still remaining profitable. Use one or a combination to increase the range of products you offer and the amount you can sell.

Driving to the supplier cuts into profits. No matter how many machines you operate and how long your vending machine company has been in business, it is important to take drive time and travel costs into account when choosing your supplier. If you drive to the location, it costs gas, potentially tolls, and wear and tear on the vehicle. Your time has value too. On the other hand, if you have products delivered, you need to take shipping costs into account.

Focus on buyer benefits. In the end, the products you choose and where you buy them from should matter primarily because of the experience you can give to those hungry or thirsty people standing in front of your machines with dollars in their hands. The main goal is always to offer top-quality products that are in demand and keep the machines well-stocked at all times.

When purchasing your product, make sure to check the expiration dates. If the product you purchase is close to expiring, it won't last long in your machine. You want to have several weeks before the product expires. As a vending operator, you need to be aware of the shelf life of your vending items so you can keep your product tasting the best. Most complaints that customers have is that their product is out of date.

There are different terms that different manufacturers use. Most manufacturers will use a phrase such as "sell by," "best by," "use by," or "best before," but this doesn't mean that the product is going to expire on that date, taste terrible, and make you sick if you consume it. Most snacks and drinks can go another few months past this date and you will hardly notice a difference. The food or beverage will gradually start to get harder and taste stale, but they won't harm you unless they are years past the date. However, your customers won't like seeing expired products in your vending machine, so take them out and offer them as freebies. Everyone loves free stuff and your location will appreciate your good customer service.

By storing your products in cool, dark areas, you can extend the life of your snacks and drinks considerably. You may have already found that it is rather difficult to find the "best by" or expiration date on many food packages. Some manufacturers only provide the date on which it was "born," while others will provide some long code of numbers and letters which will somehow relate to the manufactured date or the expiration date. Unfortunately, there is no law which standardizes how manufacturers label the shelf life of their product.

With that in mind, below is a list of popular vending items along with a general rule of how long they should be kept in circulation from the date they were manufactured. Once again, this doesn't mean that the product will be bad after this time period, it just means that the snack or beverage won't taste its best if you keep it in circulation longer.

- Chocolate candy – 9 to 12 months
- Sugary candy – 18 months
- Gumballs – 18 months
- Nuts – 6 to 10 months
- Chips – 2 to 3 months
- Pop Tarts – 5 to 7 months
- Granola Bars – 6 to 8 months
- Bottled soda – 3 to 4 months
- Canned diet soda – 3 to 4 months
- Canned non-diet soda – 9 to 12 months
- Gatorade and juice drinks – 9 to 12 months
- Water – over a year

Selling the right product to your customers is an important aspect of running a good, profitable vending business. There is not one magic list of products that will work for every location. Much testing and modifying should take place to get the right fit for each location. One method for choosing snack and drink items is to provide the location you are entering with a checklist of snacks and drinks that you commonly sell. Have the employees check the items they are most interested in seeing in their machine. You will also learn what they like and don't like by watching the sale of each product. If it sells fast, they like it; however, if it doesn't sell, they don't like it.

Other items that sell well in vending machines include school or office supplies. A snack vending machine doesn't have to only offer snacks. They can offer anything that people at the location might need. This way, people won't have to go to a convenience store and stand in line for a lone pen. At one of my vending machines I sell plastic utensils. They are big sellers there because the location does not offer utensils. So, if the employees need utensils and they forgot to bring their own, they can buy them from me. At a gym location I sell socks because people often forget their socks when they go to the gym directly from work.

If you decide to offer healthy snacks, and I recommend you offer some, don't overdo it. Many companies are asking venders to offer more healthy items. Some have been told this will help lower their health insurance cost. Since you want to keep the customer happy but can gather from others' experience good-for-you products don't often sell well, meet them partway. When I first started my vending business, I offered only healthy snacks in my machines. I had a lot of outdated products that went to waste. Even people who say they want a healthy product machine still want some less than healthy options. Over the years I have noticed that having about 20% healthy products in my machines works well for most locations.

A good approach for a vending machine operator is to supply what the customer wants, within reason. The nature of our business is to keep the customers happy. When I'm approached about adding additional healthy items, I listen. As we discuss the matter, I will usually explain in a polite way that my business must still make a profit. That usually makes them receptive as I steer them toward making these changes in small increments.

The most popular items found in my snack vending machines include chips, breakfast items, and candy bars. Some items are Snickers, Peanut M&M's, Twix, Reese's Peanut Butter Cups, KitKat, Milky Way, gum, Doritos, Cheetos, Lays Potato Chips, Oreos, Famous Amos Cookies, Rice Crispy Treats, peanuts, trail mix, honey buns, Strawberry Pop Tarts, Big Texas Danish, Cheez-its, granola bars, beef jerky, and pretzels.

The most popular drinks in my vending machines include water, Mountain Dew, energy drinks, Pepsi, Coke, Sprite, Diet Coke, Diet Pepsi, Dr Pepper, Sunkist, Jumex, and Gatorade.

Pricing

The cost of your product is important to you and your customer. Too high and your customer won't buy anything; too low and you don't make any profit. When I started my vending machine business, I was able to set the cost of candy bars at $1. This still allowed me to make 50% off each bar sold. Now candy bars are much more expensive, so charging $1.50 per bar is within the realm of what you should charge.

Products purchased for sale within the machine need to be tracked. It helps to check out different suppliers' costs every once and while. I generally use Sam's Warehouse for my purchases because they carry more of the product that my customers request. However, if I want to keep two memberships, I could go to Costco and purchase my chocolates at a lower price, or at least that was the case last time I checked.

Do I want to keep two different club warehouses memberships just for a case of M&M's that are a couple bucks cheaper? For me it's not worth it, but it may be for you. I also have to take into account the time and gas it will take to visit both warehouses each time.

Continuity of pricing is helpful to your customer. Since I charge $1 for candy, I try to make all of my products a dollar or less. That also means that people don't have to come up with change, which a lot of people don't like carrying around. Now that candy bars are $1.50, I try to keep all of the product cost under $2. I also price everything in $0.25-cent increments. This is less important on machines that accept credit cards, but people still like thinking in relatively round numbers.

If people request more expensive products, like Kind bars, you will need to price these higher than most of your other items to reflect your additional costs. You will probably find that they don't sell as well, but for good customer service you need to give the customer what they request.

To figure out how to price items, check out the price in the grocery store. A vending machine is more convenient than a grocery or convenience store, so people should expect to pay a higher price. In general, though, sales are better if the vending machine price is close to what they would expect in the grocery store, a price they are familiar with.

A general rule of thumb for pricing items is to have a 50% markup. That might sound like a lot, but these items don't cost very much, and you have to pay yourself for your time, maintenance costs, and gas. You can actually charge whatever price you want, but people might not pay it. When initially setting your prices at a new location, it is always better to start on the high side. It is psychologically better for the customer to see you bring the price down; people think they are getting a better bargain. If you set your prices low and have to raise them, you will have a lot of unhappy people. Determine the price per item, then round your price up to whatever gives you at least 50% profit.

I provide a complete chart of what I use to determine my pricing as a bonus gift to you. It is contained within the toolkit of ideas and forms which is offered as a special bonus with the purchase of this book. You can claim this bonus gift for free here: https://www.vendingbusiness-book.com/gift.

Here's an illustration of the top few columns of this Excel spreadsheet:

Item	Unit cost	Count per unit	Unit cost/count per unit	Selling price	Selling price/unit price-1	Selling price – individual cost
			This gives you cost per individual	Price set by you	Percent markup	Profit margin
Coke	9.78	35	0.28	0.75	1.68	0.47
Lays chips	12.48	30	0.42	1.00	1.4	0.58

On this table, I show that Coke costs me $9.78 for a unit of 35 cans. Each of those cans cost me 28 cents. I pick my selling price based on what other vending machines are selling their cans for, in this example the price is 75 cents. That gives me a markup of 1.68 percent and a profit margin of 47 cents. That means that for every can of Coke I sell, I make 47 cents. Lays chips cost me $12.48 for a case of 30. Each individual bag cost 28 cents. I sell them for $1.00 (in this example) and make 58 cents per bag. As you can see, you don't make huge amounts per item, but with lots of items and lots of days for people to buy them, you can make some decent money.

Storing

Products for the machines need to be stored. When I started the business, I had a large house with a garage, so that wasn't a problem at all. Later, when I sold the house to downsize, I didn't have the room to store product anymore, so I rented a climate-controlled storage unit. Climate control is necessary for chocolate so that it doesn't melt or freeze, for candy so it doesn't all mush together, for drinks so they don't burst open, and for chips so they don't go stale quickly. Life can become very messy and expensive as you weed through spoiled product representing lost income when you don't store it within the correct temperature range. The storage unit doesn't have to be very large; eight feet by eight feet area is usually plenty of room.

Product Organization

Product organization within the machine helps with sales by clustering like items together. People don't want to search around for the snack they seek. They want all of the healthy snacks in one area, all chocolate in one area, all sugary snacks in one area, all chips in one area, and breakfast items in one area.

Once you have your items divided by type, put them in the machine in an attractive order. For example, separate Reese's from KitKat using another candy like a snickers bar because the orange Reese's wrapper color clashes with the reddish orange of the KitKat wrapper color. Put brighter-colored products on the edges because they will stand out better than the darker-colored products. With chips, put smaller bags toward the sides of the machine because they are less likely to get jammed against the glass. Also, try to keep similar sizes together for aesthetic reasons. When I started, I didn't know these details, so I had breakfast items mixed in with chips. However, once I separated them, my breakfast item sales increased.

Keep like-sized products together. There are several different configurations for displaying products in vending machines, but vendors generally keep chips on the top two rows. One row for bigger bags and the other row for smaller bags. If you intermix large and small bags, the customers will often purchase only the bigger bags thinking they are getting a better deal; this is fine except when your smaller bagged items expire because no one is purchasing them.

Pastries should go on the third row if you have a location with a bunch of men. To generalize, locations with men tend to like pastries first thing in the morning, so you will want to put the pastries where they can easily find them. The next row should hold the chocolate, especially if the location has mostly women. Yes, I'm generalizing again. The reason I chose the fourth row for chocolate is because most vending machine conformations have the narrower rows on the fourth and fifth shelves. On the fifth shelf, I usually put the Nabisco crackers, small packets of peanuts, Skittles, Paydays, and healthy options. If there are additional shelves, you can have a gum and mint row, or whatever else you want to add to your machine.

CHAPTER 9

Provide Great Service

The number of machines you visit per day depends on the spread of your locations and how many machines are at each location. I separate my locations by region. I lump Durham, Hillsboro, and Chapel Hill in one group: The North Group. Raleigh and Knightdale are in another group: The East Group. RTP, Cary, and Morrisville represent the third group: The South/West Group.

After you have your locations lumped by area, you will need to consider where your supplier is located. If you have a good storage area, this won't be as important. A few years ago, I had a Sam's Club in each of my areas. This worked perfect for me, but then Sam's closed a store, so I had to adjust. Because of the number of my machines, I visit my product warehouse every day. I have a Toyota Sienna eight-seat van without any of the back seats in it, so I can fill it enough to service all of the locations I visit for that day.

As you can see, you have to plan, think, and work to earn your money. Once you have your route defined and your suppliers lined up, you are ready to visit your locations. There you'll want to provide amazing service, so you are able to keep your vending accounts.

Keep Your Machines Well Maintained

The key to a properly functioning vending machine is preventative maintenance. Machine service depends on usage. Some locations will go through the available food quickly, so they will need to be serviced more often. Some will not be as quick with the turnover of food and drink. In general, I service my machines once per week. If they have a lower usage, I visit every other week. If they need me more often than once per week, that means they need a bigger machine or more machines. Until I can put a different machine in that location, I will visit it as often as necessary.

Keeping your machine clean is very important for the continued happiness of both your machine and your customers. I carry window cleaner, rags, money bags, tape, pen, business cards, scissors and occasionally a Phillips head screwdriver and pliers to each location. These items are stored in a strong bag I carry over my shoulder. Once I chat with whomever is by the machine to find out if they have had any problems, I clean the windows and any surfaces that are dirty. Next, I take the money out of both the coin and dollar bill areas and put the money in a labeled bag for that specific machine. At this time, I also add any coinage that is needed. Often, quarters and $1 coins need to be added to the machine if people use $5 bills to pay for their products.

Check all of the products still in the machine for expiration dates and remove any item that is expired or will be within the week. I generally leave the products that I take out of the machine on a table where people can come by and get a free goody. Then, you'll want to straighten up all of the remaining products and add more as needed.

If your chips are sticking, you will need to use Goof-off to remove the residue under the coils. If an item isn't vending properly, you need to figure out why that is happening. Generally, your customers will tell you if a row isn't vending; however, it is a good idea to test vend every row once a month. Also, check your pricing and other settings on all of your machines once a month because sometimes power outages can disrupt your settings.

Engage with Your Customers

Customers will give you other suggestions of what to put in the machine while you are at your location. They will also tell you about what it is selling and what isn't, in their opinion. Before you change out any items, you need to check your machine to confirm a product isn't selling, just in case the customer's interpretation of what is or isn't selling is incorrect. Is the product really not selling or is the person just not seeing anyone eating or drinking it?

When you add a new product or switch out items, make sure they replace your worst sellers. I have found that Peanut M&M's and Snickers are purchased and highly sought after in every location. The only locations that I don't have those two items in are machines in locations that specifically asked me not to add them.

Freebies are good and appreciated but not always necessary. When I take non-sellers out at low-selling locations, I put them in a more productive machine, as long as they aren't expired. If they are expired, I usually take them to a highly productive location to leave them as free treats for my best customers.

Keep communication positive. Be proactive and responsive. Stay in touch with your contact at the location. Most of my contacts are not the people I see when I visit the machines. A call is a good way to stay in touch. Get feedback from your customers and your contact and be personable while talking to them.

Lastly, take all of your packaging (trash) out with you. If your contact has personally stated that you can leave your trash on the premises, they usually change their mind within a few weeks. It's better to avoid what feels like a complaint once people realize how much garbage results from a vending route. Take responsibility right from the start for carrying away your packaging.

Machine Cleaning

While soapy water is recommended for cleaning vending equipment, there are other cleaning brands that will help keep machines clean. The choice is up to you. Regardless of what type of cleaner you choose, here are some best practices for cleaning vending equipment.

Recommended supplies:

- Disposable non-linting cloths
- Clean disposable gloves
- Plastic scraper
- Spray bottle w/ cleaning solution
- Glass cleaner or similar product for cleaning the window

Ensure the machine is switched off before completing any cleaning tasks. Do not apply or spray the soapy water solution directly onto surfaces that could or might leak directly onto electrical components such as the keypad or touch screen. Where this is a possibility, wring out a soapy clean cloth and then use this clean cloth to wipe the surface.

Using three separate cloths (contact, mostly clean, and mostly dirty) is an additional recommendation since the coronavirus pandemic. I used to have just two: one for wiping mostly clean areas and one for dirty area cleaning. The 'contact' cloth is used to clean the areas of the machine that your customers touch, such as the keypad and the change return area. The 'mostly clean' cloth is used on internal areas of the machine. The 'mostly dirty' cloth is used on all external surfaces with the exception of areas of the machine that are exposed to consumer interactions.

Some Do's and Don'ts:

- Always wear protective gloves
- Always use the correct cleaning agent for the application and follow the manufacturer's instructions
- Make sure the machine is powered down before cleaning
- Do not use water on the electronic components
- Do not use metal scrapers to clean the gunk off rows, use something like Goof Off
- Do not put any of the machine's internal parts on the floor

Machine maintenance is quick and easy if you keep a regular cleaning schedule. Before you leave your location, make sure the machine is powered back on and everything is working. When powering on the machine, you will hear the clicking and whirling of the bill acceptors, change mechanism, and the credit card reader if you have one on the machine. If you don't hear all of those mechanisms making a sound, make sure the machine is really on and all of the connections are secure in the electronic area.

Additional cleaning and maintenance are required on occasion. There is a certain amount of care and maintenance that needs to be done for a large purchase like a vending machine. Just like purchasing a home or a vehicle, vending machines are an investment and should be treated as such. Improper use and neglect will cause lower productivity which will lead to a loss of profit. Below are parts of the vending machine that require this a few times per year.

Refrigeration deck, the area of a drink or freezer machine where the compressor is housed. Clean the refrigeration air intake coils (condenser) every 2-4 months. The condenser is normally located at the very bottom of the machine and accessed from the front; however, on some models it is accessed from the back of the machine.

For the front located compressors, you will need to remove the protective metal kick-plate which you can locate by looking for the air intake slits or holes. The back located compressor often doesn't have a protective plate. This plate usually just lifts off but may be attached to the unit with screws. Then, use a brush, broom, or vacuum to remove any heavy accumulation of lint. It also may be necessary to use compressed air to clear fine dirt/dust particles from the condenser itself. You might also want to have a pail of soapy water to wipe down any dirty surfaces. After cleaning is complete, you can remount the kick-plate to the vending machine.

Bill validator, where the bills are collected in the machine. The bill validator should be cleaned every 30 to 60 days, depending on use. Always turn off the power to the vending machine before cleaning. Start by removing the cash box, where the bills are collected. Clean the box with a clean dry cloth. Next, remove the sensor tray, located above or below the cash box. This will normally pull out by depressing the two tabs on the sides of the box or pressing a tab on the bottom. Clean the sensor tray with a clean, dry cloth. If it is extremely dirty, you can wring out a soapy cloth until damp to clean the tray. Always dry the tray when complete.

Surge protector. Always plug your machine into a surge protector and not just a power strip! Most surge protectors will have a resettable test button or switch. Test the protector every so often to make sure it is working properly. If it has a switch, turn the switch off to make sure it cuts power to the vending machine. When testing in either of these two cases, if power to the vending machine is not cut, replace the surge protector.

Coin units, where the coins are housed within the machine. The coin unit tubes should be filled 2/3 of the way for starting a new machine; they will completely fill as the machine is used. The coin units should be cleaned every 30 to 60 days, depending on use. Always turn off the power to the vending machine before cleaning. Clean the coin inlet with a clean, dry cloth. If it is extremely dirty, you can wring out a soapy cloth, then clean the tray. Always dry the tray when complete. Clean the coin run on the mechanism side and door side. Always check for broken or missing parts while cleaning.

Drink/Snack vending mechanism which are the coils that dispense the product. Check for proper drink/snack vending operation every time you load a new product or every 60 to 90 days. Enter the machines service mode and perform a motor test to vend (or dispense) your product to ensure there are no issues.

Normally, there are little to no issues with vending snacks. If the snacks (usually chips) stick on the tray you will need to clean that tray with either a soapy cloth or a product like Goof Off. Drinks may have vending problems due to bottle/can size and the total weight associated with the drinks when fully loaded. Always test vend with one to three bottles/cans before fully loading the machine. Then test again once all of the products are loaded. If drinks don't vend properly, check the delivery mechanism for binding or minimize the number of products you add to the row. Many drink companies thin their containers to save money; if the product package is thinned too much they can get squished together and won't vend properly; water bottles are bad for this. Or, with cans, if the packaging is too thin they can explode in the machine. This happened in 2019 when both Coke and Pepsi thinned their packaging too much. Currently, the water bottles with the thickest package are Deer Park 20-oz bottles. Even with this brand of water you can only put in half of the product that the machine should be able to hold.

Make sure you use a proper sized shim if needed. The shim is a piece that you can put into the rotating part of the drink machine to make sure your drinks are snug in the dispensing unit. Vending machines are set to vend a certain sized product such as a 20oz soda or standard can size. If you want to vend a skinny product such as a Red Bull, you need to insert a shim to make up the space. If you don't do this, the skinnier product will get stuck in the delivery mechanism and won't vend.

Lastly, make sure the product is loaded properly, the sold-out sensors work properly, and there are no motor issues such as failure or stripped gears.

By following these basic routine maintenance tasks, you can help to extend the life of your vending machine and ensure maximum productivity. If at any time a machine is not working properly, refer to the machine's owner manual or call a vending repair professional in order to receive a proper diagnosis and guidance on how to fix the problem.

CHAPTER 10

Look Inside: A Day in the Life of a Successful Vending Machine Entrepreneur

The typical day in the life of a vending machine operator begins with writing down all of the locations you need to visit. I have my locations separated by area and I service one area per day. Each area consists of locations that are close together. Since I have 50 machines, I have approximately 10 machines per area. That does not mean that I visit 10 locations per area, though, because some locations have more than one machine. One of my locations has four machines. I also try to visit my locations on the same day of the week each week because my locations appreciate the regularity.

Next, I inventory the product bins, coolers, chips and drinks for today's route. You'll want to write down everything that these specific locations need that you don't have, based on their current use. I store my chocolates in a cooler year-round. This helps keep the chocolates at a steady temperature whether it is freezing or boiling outside. The bins are used for storing all product that don't melt, other than chips. I use four 50-gallon tubs to load all of the non-chip snacks. One tub has healthy snacks, another tub has the $0.50 items, another has M&M's and Skittles along with similar candy, and the fourth is used for pastries and breakfast items.

Load your inventoried bins and coolers filled with product into your car. Also, load drinks and chips. Try to load in an organized fashion so that it's easy to access everything and nothing gets squashed.

Then drive to your product storage location if you have one and fill up on needed inventory. If you don't have everything you need for the day, drive to your supplier to fill in the gaps.

On the visits to your locations, restock and service your machine. Every visit to a machine should include cleaning the windows, emptying the coins and bills, wiping down the outside and cleaning the parts of the machine that your customers regularly touch such as the touch pad and coin return. Also conduct whatever maintenance is required at that time.

The last business for the day is accounting for all of your financial intake. Yes, this is where the fun begins. Every time I visit a location I collect the coins and dollars from the machine and keep this money in labeled bags. The labels indicate the location and individual machine. For money storage, I just use plastic Ziplock bags that I keep in my canvas bag. Once I reach home, I count the money in each bag and record the amount on a spreadsheet so I can track each machine and each location's financial intake.

To make this a bit easier, I have a coin rack to help with the coins. These racks provide the right amount of space for rolled coin wrappers. That means it has space for fifty pennies, $2 in nickels, $5 for dimes, a $10 quarter space, and room for $25 of dollar coins in each slot. I add the coin to the slot and once the slot is filled to the proper level for a coin wrapper, I take the coins out and put them in the sleeves. For the bills, I count them in piles of ten. When the bills equal $100 for $1s, and $500 for $5s, I wrap them in a bill wrapper. You can get bill and coin wraps from the bank that holds your business account. Lastly, I add the bills and coins up and put that number in the proper area of my spreadsheet. Some local banks will wrap the coins for you. If they will do that for you, you'll save a lot of time during your accounting.

The easiest way to keep all of the money recorded is to count and record the money on a spreadsheet for the day of collection. This way, you can see how profitable each machine and each location is at any given time. This will also help when scheduling your next visit. If the machine only made $10 during the week, either you won't need to visit that machine again for a couple weeks, or you need to switch out your snacks and drinks for products the customers like better, or you need to find a different location.

Money needs to be monitored for every machine from every location for whichever date you collect the money. In the example below I visit location A, C, and D on Monday the 1st. At location A, I have two machines and I record the snack first and drink second. On Tuesday I visit location B and E, which each have one machine.

Month	Location	Location A snack/drink	Location B	Location C	Location D	Location E
Day	Date					
Monday	1	$56.50/$24		32.70	25.40	
Tuesday	2		78.30			112.25

At the end of each month, I list the totals per location and total for the month. These figures help when paying your sales and use tax.

I provide a complete excel form of what I use to monitor my machines as a bonus gift to you. It is contained within the toolkit of ideas and forms which is offered as a special bonus with the purchase of this book. You can claim this bonus gift for free here: https://www.VendingBusinessBook.com/gift

You also need to track the various costs and information that you accrue with every purchase of a vending machine. Include the following information on your spreadsheet:

- Machine make and model
- Card reader serial number, if applicable
- Current machine location
- Current area within the location where the machine is located
- Location address
- Name and number of the contact person at the location
- Machine purchase date
- Location installation date – record every machine relocation date for the life of the machine
- Machine cost

This information can be used when you call the machine manufacturer or repair person with an issue they need to help you diagnose and resolve. It will also come in handy when you are ready to sell your machine, your buyers will want to see this information. Plus, you will never forget your contact person's name or the location.

Below is a summarized sample of how you might use my machine information tracking spreadsheet. The first machine was purchased and moved to a location on the same day. The second machine stayed in my garage for a couple months, then moved to a location. And the third machine was moved from an old location to a new location. The old location information was moved to the far right of the spreadsheet, so I still have that information available for future reference.

Make, Model Serial #	Current Location	Area	Purchase Date	Installation Date	Machine Cost
Crane 146	A	Break room	1/20/14	1/20/14	$7,000
National 252	B	Front Hall	7/3/18	10/2/18	$6,500
USI 325	C	Gym	8/2/16	1/12/18	$5,500

When you give away products for promotion or simply to thank customers at a particularly lucrative location, keep track of that cost so you can write it off on your taxes. Also track outdated and bad product for tax purposes. Product expiration dates are important to track because you never want to have expired product in your machine.

Either your vehicle expenses (this includes car payments, gasoline, maintenance, repairs, registration, etc.) or your car's mileage need to be tracked for tax purposes. If you choose to log actual costs, you'll need to calculate what percentage of your driving is for business vs. personal if it's not exclusively a company car. Generally, tracking mileage is easier as long as you keep business and personal mileage separate. During tax time you can write off the cost of either but need to use the method you pick consistently.

CHAPTER 11

Grow, Expand, and Scale

Grow

To grow your business, you need a methodical approach. Start with writing out your specific goals as discussed in Chapter 2. I have grown my business as large as I can handle alone and still be able to take a couple vacations a year. This objective is reflected in my goals and associated strategies.

As your business grows, your vehicle will need to grow. I started with a Toyota RAV4; now I have an eight-seat Toyota Sienna with all of the back seats removed. If I did my own machine moving, or grew larger, I would want a truck with a hydraulic lift.

As you grow and build your locations and routes, sooner or later your business will peak. Once you reach the point where if you purchase one more machine your service to all of your machines will suffer, you have to make the decision of what your next step will be.

One choice is to stay as a one-person operation and keep servicing all of the machines you have. This includes purchasing new machines as the old ones die and adding new locations as old locations disappear.

One of your best sales tools for growth is to increase the demand for product in each machine you've already placed. Let your potential customers know about the presence of your vending machines. If your customers do not know about the availability of your vending machine and the products it vends, you will not reap any profits. Make the most of your advertisements by including images of the vending machines with details of their locations. Mention the services and products your machines offer. Social networking is a great way to reach your customers. Let them know about the new products and updated machines.

A second way to move forward is to sell your machine route to another party, hopefully for a profit. Then you can use that profit for some other business opportunity or to fund your next round of building routes and placing vending machines in new locations. Basically, you are spending money to reach a certain level of business with your machines and then selling the business for a nice little profit. The great part about doing this is the ability to manage and run everything by yourself, with little to no need for any extra help as you find and put together a smaller number of locations over and over again. It also allows for a faster and more immediate profit bump.

The problem with selling your business over and over is that the route needs to develop into a smooth and steady income flow before it has any chance of being a tempting buy. In order to be able to sell the route for what you believe it to be worth, you need to do a lot of work and research to prove to the local buyer that it's worth the cost. Also, that potential profit which they're getting from purchasing your business route could have been yours.

A third choice is to expand into new areas, markets, products, and perhaps services. This will require hiring employees and increasing the overhead in other aspects of your business. The benefit of continuing with expansion while keeping all of your machines serviced and running well is a much higher return in money over the long run. But as your company gets bigger, there is more investing needed, more machines to buy and handle, and more people to hire and manage.

The effort can be rewarding, but it needs a lot of work to develop and prosper.

The final choice is yours and depends on your long-term hopes and goals. If you are looking to sell, then find a local buyer. Show them the advantages of purchasing your existing business, such as having the locations close together for time and gas savings and a loyal, established customer base. Share your unique ideas to keep the route prosperous or make it better. Then you can sell the business and do something else. But if you'd like to continue to grow, then there are some actions to consider.

Find locations, again! The importance of finding locations has already been touched upon a few times. There should be no need for a reminder that one should always be looking for new locations, but I'm going to say it again anyway. This is especially true if you're using the second option listed above and building solidly made routes over and over to sell them for a profit. All of these routes will need new locations. Procuring locations will lead to a successful long-running vending business.

Finding locations continually is necessary to build profit and income sources for the year, but there's an even more important reason to make new location prospecting a priority. The fact remains, no matter how tasty and popular your snacks are, or how polished your business and customer skills, none of your machine locations will last forever.

The time your machines spend in each location is finite. There will always be some reason or time when your machine will need to be moved. Perhaps your machine no longer does well with local crowds, or the trends change from vending machines to mini-markets. Other factors affecting the value or appropriateness of current locations include discovering a site is too dangerous or, the building gets sold, renovated, or taken down. As for when this will occur, it varies, lasting anywhere from six months to twenty plus years.

To continue increasing your business, you will probably need to expand your location circle. Look for similar locations further away. Eventually, you will need to add employees and an office to cover the increased distance. Also, you could go back and look at old locations that originally didn't work out for one reason or another. After some time in the business, having proven your vending business is successful and well-liked by customers in your current locations, head back to a location contact who previously said no and show them the work that you've done. You never know, they could change their mind.

You can also put your machines in locations that you thought wouldn't be profitable. The location's demographics might have changed, there might be new businesses around that location, or you might have added improvements to your own product offerings. Many options can and will open up the longer your business remains operational.

Expand by Hiring Employees

The more your business demand increases and the more machines you add to your route, the more likely it is that you will need more people, more product, and extra help. You'll only be able to continue going out and doing everything yourself for so long. At some point, you will need to delegate some of your work, so you have time to handle orders, organization, and future business management. Initially, you will probably hire one or two people to drive around to refill and take inventory of machines. After a while more intense jobs will need to be filled, like sending others to research potential locations, presenting sales pitches, and taking in product orders. Ultimately, the tasks that you want to hand out to others and keep for yourself is up to you; it will become clear over time which tasks you need to keep for yourself to ensure a successfully run business.

Eventually, you'll want a manager to help run some of the same inventory and sales-keeping tasks you used to perform. You might need them to go out in the field, or simply direct the other new employees, and even handle the actual hiring process for you. This will leave you free to run the bigger aspects of the business and be selective about the duties you choose.

There are two options for hiring a manager. One is to slowly train a trustworthy employee who has demonstrated good work habits. This is a great approach when you have the time and employees available. The second alternative is to hire someone who has proven themselves at other businesses and can manage vending machine employees.

As for the actual hiring, there are multiple resources where you can place listings for potential job seekers, such as Monster, Indeed, and Career Builder. Take into consideration that some of these sites cost money for advertisement placement. Another option is to use Craigslist to look for employees; it's absolutely free, there are plenty of people who look at those listings, and it's easy to setup. However, you will have to re-post the listing every couple of days.

If you are having trouble getting applicants or hiring the right employee, you can have others find them. You can work with temp agencies, external/contingency recruiters, or headhunters. They can more easily find the right people for the positions you need filled. Depending on what agencies and particular services you are looking for, the cost is variable. A good type of recruiter to consider are contingency recruiters; they only get paid if their applicants are hired.

Another expansion idea is to open an office in another area. While increasing and expanding your business reach, your machine locations will be further away, perhaps so far away that you don't want to drive to them every week. This is when you might want to consider opening an office in that region. At that office you will have a manager who hires additional staff from that area to fill and maintain the machines.

A few items you will want to take into account include the extra cost involved in opening another office, including rent and salaries. You will need to decide if an office is cost effective. Are you making enough profit in the distant locations and will you be saving an adequate amount in expenses to justify the money spent to keep an office? When expanding your business into different areas, cities, and even states, also be aware of the local regulations for shipping, storage, and buildings. The differences will not be large, but it is always a good idea to check to avoid any difficulties later on.

To expand your business, you can also look for new ideas and products. Everything in the world changes eventually, including your business realities. You have to be adaptable to the changes to be successful. You cannot expect to offer the exact same product from the same machine over the decades and keep growing, let alone stay profitable. Not only can area demographics change, but locations can also open or close.

Increase the scale of your business by staying up to date on trends, popular interests, advancements, and issues in terms of food service. This is important not just for identifying obstacles to navigate, but also for locating resources that you can utilize in your business. If you operate a classic snack, soda, and other multiple-choice vending machine business, be on the lookout for new products that can be placed into your machines. Notice the kinds of flavors and products that are popular in the media and try those new items in your machines. I often find that sales increase on products that are currently being advertised on TV. For instance, when Reese's Peanut Butter Cups are advertised, I often have up to a 50% increase in sales.

Also, look into replacing some of the regular items in your machine for diversity. Keep the machine interesting and exciting. Find out what products will complement your current stock. Perhaps add a different brand of chip, or different type of cookie. Just remember that if you go too far off the well-known brands your customers won't want to try them; you can help to avoid this problem by offering freebies of the new items.

Another idea is to diversify the location. If vending machines in an area are vending hot food, you could vend snacks, or cold drinks. Think from the users' point of view and you will get lots of great ideas. The future of your vending business is determined by scaling the business size up higher, and also by being able to adjust to the current wants and needs of your customer.

Upgrading your machines can also expand your business. Technological improvements are being made constantly, and new updated machines are produced every year. Customers appreciate more attractive vending options. Location managers also appreciate new machines and different products; they are more likely to let you replace a vending competitors old, outdated, and ugly machine with your new, fresh, and fun machines. Another way to upgrade at your current locations is to add different types of machines. This is an excellent way to go especially if you have to refill your current machine more than once per week. By switching out a smaller machine with a bigger machine or adding another machine with different options you won't need to visit the location as often, saving you time and money.

Another way to upgrade the scale of your business is to upgrade your machines with newer technology. You can contact the manufacturer of your current machine, give them the serial number, and they can tell you if your machine is credit card capable. If it is, you can purchase a credit card reader and install it in your old machine. If your old machine is not credit card able you can replace your old machine for one that is. Customers who want cashless, credit, and debit cards, or just like new things, will then start using your machine more often.

As an entrepreneur who wants to expand your business and increase your earnings you need to have a plan. Always think from the users' point of view. This will help you find the right ways to offer what they want. By reading the trade magazines such as Vending Times, you can keep up with the latest trends and advancements. This will help you to discover popular ways to upgrade your vending machines and vending options.

CHAPTER 12

The Good, the Bad, and the Ugly

Yes, all of these things exist in any business, but most aren't listed in a concise way that's easy for you to understand and apply to your circumstances.

The Good

You are your own boss. This was covered earlier in the book along with some of reasons this can be a good thing. Owning a business gives you flexibility that lets you decide how you're going to make as much or as little money as you want. Another reason being your own boss is a good thing is that you can pull out of a location if you don't like it or the people you're dealing with are just getting on your nerves. In the contract that you sign with your location make sure you request at least a 30-day notice before either you or the location can move the machine. This will protect both parties giving you time to plan the transition and them time to make adjustments.

An example of this occurred with my business when I purchased a route with a machine that only produced $20 per month net. I had to drive 30 miles to this location each time I needed to service or repair the machine. I spoke to my contact at the property about how not making enough money posed a problem for keeping the machine at the location. I offered to let them pay me a $50 fee per visit for my time, gas, and effort as an alternative to moving the machine to a more profitable location. My contact thought that was a great idea; unfortunately, the management did not agree.

Can set your own timetable. Grow as large as you want, at whatever pace you want. I wanted to have time to learn as I grew and felt that growing by 10 machines a year was the way to go. However, when I had the opportunity and finances to purchase a route, I grew by 15 machines in one day. That made for a very busy and hectic month. I had to work longer hours to get all of the machines producing at a level I was happy with, but it was definitely worth the time and effort financially.

Work as little or as much as you want. I like to visit relatives for a week every year. I set the summer as a time for my visit because that is when school is out so the machines that I have in schools will not be active. The week before my vacation I visit every location and make sure they are filled and running smoothly. The week after my vacation I do the same. This means that all of my locations that I visit once every two weeks don't notice any change. For the machines I visit once or twice a week, I notify them that I will be out of town and service their machines the day before my vacation and again the day after.

Another reason working as much or as little as you want is a good thing is because sometimes you just don't feel like working. In a job you could take a personal day, but that is usually frowned upon. As a self-employed businessperson, if you want to take a day off, go ahead. You will have to work harder on other days to make up for the time off, but on the day you didn't want to work you didn't have to.

Meet a lot of different people. Every location is different in people and personality. Office building people are usually very focused on their work and rarely want to chat. School teachers' lounges have teachers on break who might be chatty or might be having a rough day. Manufacturing plant people are usually the friendliest. They are happy to see more snacks delivered and want to chat if they are on break. Medical facilities are also happy to see you and are the most likely to tell you about any problems with the machine. A mostly male facility will want more drinks and chips. Whereas, a mostly female facility will want more diet soda and chocolate. People from different countries, backgrounds, and cultures all have their own preferences so you can meet them and figure out what those preferences are.

At one of my locations, I met and befriended a person from Zimbabwe. It has been wonderful getting to learn about the culture there and more about this person. At another location I have a friend from Guatemala. Hearing about their life stories has been fascinating. I also have a location that is an assisted living facility. Once I thought I might have broken my wrist in a fall outside of the facility and a gentleman there who used to be an orthopedic surgeon was able to look and feel my wrist and assure me that it was just a severe strain. In that case, it was nice to meet a wonderful person and also save on a co-pay.

Make money without being on site constantly. It is nice to wake up in the morning and know that your machine has been handling business for you. This passive income helps you to be able to have multiple machines making money. Most of my locations have credit card readers that allow me to remotely monitor my machines to see how much they're earning in real time. I also have some locations that don't want card readers for one reason or another. At those locations, I am often surprised by the amount of money I collect. Yeah, I shouldn't be that surprised since all sales are done with cash, but because most of my machines have credit card readers, it's still fun having all of that money come out of the machine.

Most of your clients will be thrilled to see you. "Yeah, the snack lady is here!!!" "Here comes cookie lady." I've been called several names along those lines. For a while, I thought of putting my name in big letters on my shirt so people could call me by my name, but snack and cookie lady works fine. I like being wanted. Sometimes, when I'm having a blah day, I get a real lift from hearing someone say how wonderful it is that I am there.

Vend what and where you want. If you want to vend socks in a gym vending machine, just make sure it can vend from the row where you place it and that it can be retrieved from the product drawer. One of my locations is a factory where the employees don't have access to utensils with which to eat their meals. So, I purchased a box of the combo plastic utensil packs and sell the utensils in the same machine as the snacks. They buy out the row every couple of weeks. Plastic utensils have a great mark up. You can purchase a box of 100 utensil sets for $12, that is 8.3 cents each. Then turn around and sell each set for $0.35, that is a $0.27 profit for each set sold. That's over a 90% mark up.

The Bad

There is a ***limitation*** to how many machines you can service on your own without hiring an employee. I have found that my limit is around 50 machines to be able to take care of all of them with good customer service. If you do want to run more machines, you could try hiring temporary employees like students, but they won't have the dedication that you do, and your customer service might not be as good.

Not everything can be vended out of your machine. You need to test run a product. This includes going through the entire process from loading to the customers' purchase experience. Does it fit properly between the coils when you load it? Make sure it isn't too large for the product drawer. If there are any issues, don't place it in your machine. Once I tried to vend cup-a-soup and it vended great, but I couldn't get it out of the product drawer without destroying it.

The less you work the less you make. Let's say you get sick for a week and can't service your machines. They will last for a while, but empty spaces will occur, people will run out of their favorite snacks and drinks, and products will expire. If there isn't anything they want to eat or drink available, you lose sales, which means you lose money. Again, you can hire someone else to run your route temporarily, but they probably won't take care of everything the way you do, so your customers might not be as happy.

Locations are not permanent. As I mentioned earlier, finding locations can be difficult, but you have to do it on a regular basis. Once I went 6 months with no machine moves. Usually I have a move every other month for one reason or another. The reason for this lack of permanence is because locations are filled with people and businesses. Some people are difficult to deal with, so you want to move your machine away. Some locations want the newest machine possible and if you can't give them a new machine, they will find someone else. Some businesses don't produce enough cash to justify having a new machine or even any machine. And if you are not making enough money at a location it is time to move on.

You have to constantly be on the lookout for locations. If you are providing great service to your customers, word of mouth might be enough to give you new locations as needed. How this works is as follows: Company A calls Company B (where you service their machine) and asks if they are happy with your vending service. Assuming you are giving Company B good service, they will recommend you to Company A and you will have a new location.

Keeping a website and Facebook page for your business will also help you obtain new locations because many people do a Google search to find vending machine operators; they will only call you if they see you in that search. If you do not need a new location at the time someone calls you to ask for a machine placement, you can always sell that location to another vendor.

It's a good idea to always be on the lookout for better locations too. Better can mean many things. A new location might make more money for you, or be closer to you, or have nicer people, or have a higher need for multiple machines.

Moving a machine will cost you money. A good moving and repair person is needed unless you do everything yourself. If you do everything yourself it's a good idea to invest in a truck with a lift gate or rent a covered truck with a lift gate. You will also need a hand truck that can carry over 800 pounds, a strong and sturdy platform that can hold more than 800 pounds, a strong palate lift and anything else that might help you lift a heavy machine. Drink machines should not be carried at an angle of more than 45 degrees, so they need to stand up when transferred. Also, the machine can weigh over 1,000 pounds. Always empty your machines before you move them.

If you hire a vending machine mover person, you pay for his time, expertise, and mileage. Usually the cost is around $300 per move. Having a professional move your machines has the advantage of them placing the machine in the specific area the location requires. They handle the machine with minimal tilting and bumping, and they will often balance the machine feet, so the machine is steady and does not rock.

Some customers will nitpick everything. "My chips expire today; I want my money back." "I lost 5 cents in the machine; I want my money back." A more reasonable complaint is that something didn't vend. If that is the problem, offer the person the product as replacement if possible. Sometimes the customer wants the cash but giving them the product saves you some money due to your markup of the product. If someone found an expired product, thank them for telling you and explain that you usually catch products before they expire so you can remove them and that this was an unusual oversite (and make sure this is true). Then give them a non-expired product of their choice.

Vacations have to be carefully planned so your machines are not neglected. This was covered in the "Good" section too because it has good sides and bad sides.

Machines break down occasionally. Even keeping everything well maintained isn't enough to keep a machine running. The most common failures I have seen deal with the compressor, bill validator, coin mechanism, and mother board. With all of these breakdowns you can choose to fix them yourself or call in a vending machine repair man.

Usually I can figure out what is wrong with everything except the compressor. For the compressor problems I almost always bring in a vending machine repair person. Compressors are heavy and difficult to remove from a machine, difficult to lift, difficult to put in your car, difficult to send out for repair. For me it is worth the money to have someone else deal with the problem. That being said, I always keep a spare compressor in stock so that the machine continues working while it's compressor is out for repair.

When doing a repair yourself, you can call the machine manufacturer to find out how to complete the repair, or you can find a YouTube video that shows the problem being fixed. There are also Facebook sites such as vending nation and full line vending where other vending machine operators give tips and answer machine repair questions.

Most things that break in a vending machine can be replaced. If the dollar validator is broken, take it out and replace it with one that works. You can send the broken part off to a vending machine parts repair company. If the mother board is the problem, take it out and put in one that works. This also brings up the point that you should keep some of the common parts in stock for the occasional break down. I like to keep a generator, coin mech, bill validator, and mother board in stock to minimize the machine's down time.

In general, if you can repair your computer and other things around the house, you can repair a vending machine. If you are not able to repair your machine yourself, you can ask other vendors for names of people who they recommend for fixing your machines.

The Ugly

Some used machines are very dirty. One of my first used vending machine purchases was of a very old drink machine that had dried on sticky soda spillage in it. Yuck! The machine only cost $800 and it worked, so I bought it. But cleaning it took some time. Most dirty machines can be cleaned with soap and water. Sometimes I have needed to use Goof Off.

Once I purchased a vending route filled with machines that hadn't been well maintained. Everything worked, but I don't think the glass fronts had ever been cleaned. This was also a cheap purchase, so I felt that the cleaning was well worth the cost. The nice thing that came out of this purchase is that, once I cleaned everything up, my sales increased. Since I purchased the route based on machine age and previous sales, after clean up I increased the value of the route substantially.

Some locations are very messy. One of my old locations was a service garage. The garage had never been swept or cleaned in any way that I could see. I didn't stay there for long. It had been part of the dirty route I purchased, so I cleaned up the machine and found a better location. Currently I have a paving garage shop that is dirty simply because of the work they have to do in the shop. At this location I clean the machine more frequently to keep the machine in good working order.

Some of the people you interact with are not friendly. Being your own boss allows you to leave these locations quickly. There is no reason to put up with unfriendly people if you can help it. One of my old machine locations had a person who complained about every little thing. Once a product was going to expire within the following week and they wanted their money back because it was too close to expiration.

Repairs can become very dirty and difficult. This is why you should have a vending machine repair person in your contact list. Also, have a few vending machine sales companies as well as a few other repair people on your contact list for reference during the difficult and messy repairs.

Some companies that sell you their product sometimes make mistakes. When Coke and Pepsi started thinning the cans in which they sold the soda they went too thin and my soda cans started exploding in my machines. That was a huge mess. Thankfully, the companies realized what was happening and thickened the cans just enough so that didn't happen anymore.

Some locations start out good, then turn bad. I was located in an apartment complex and the profits were very good. However, when the apartment complex changed management the quality of the residents took a turn for the worse and the place became dirty and wasn't being kept up. One day I visited the location and found that some riff raff had tipped my machine over and had kicked at the window trying to get free product. I quickly moved out of that location.

CHAPTER 13

Post-Pandemic Thoughts and Concerns

As I am writing this book it is late 2020, and here in the U.S., we have experienced a pandemic since the spring of this year. Life will never be the same, at least that's how it looks right now. Even if things do return to normal, there will probably be another pandemic around the corner, so it's nice to keep the new lessons learned during COVID-19 in mind.

Businesses are changing their operations and procedures to keep employees and customers safe. Providing food and beverages safely are among their biggest concerns. Federal and State governments, along with the CDC, are encouraging social distancing, including reducing or eliminating face-to-face encounters. In workplaces many are re-evaluating how food and beverages are offered to employees. Many companies are considering long-term strategies for cafeterias to help prevent the spread of COVID-19 and other infectious diseases with alternative options such as contactless delivery and self-serve options – vending machines.

These concerns have caused many organizations to evaluate self-serve convenience service options (mini markets) throughout their organizations. The risks in these venues is that the food and beverage products can be picked-up and returned to the shelves for the next consumer to handle. With COVID-19 having up to a three-day lifespan on items such as bottled beverages and salad containers, mini markets may now pose the risk of being a spreading point within organizations[14].

Mini markets have been eating into the vending machine industry lately. However, vending machines have become a better solution post-pandemic. Unlike mini markets, where consumers can touch and return the food and drink products, vending machines require the customer to purchase their chosen product without touching first. You will never know how many people have handled the product you want to purchase at the mini market.

Along with the product possibly being handled by multiple people in a mini market, another consideration is the cleanliness of the market hardware. When consumers access the products they often come in contact with the shelving holding the product. That gives the customer a risk of direct exposure on the shelf, as well as from the product. This is not a concern or risk with a vending machine, because only the operator has fully secured access to the interior of the machine.

The NIH and CDC indicates the coronavirus' lifespan on surfaces is as follows:

- Airborne: 30 minutes to 3 hours
- Cardboard: 24 hours
- Stainless Steel: 2 days
- Plastic: 3 days

According to the National Merchandising Association (NAMA), "Through our unique food distribution system, our industry can be the greatest source of contactless nourishment to over 40 million consumers with food and beverages daily, and it is all accomplished in an unattended retail environment, often with round the clock availability."[15]

According to the European Vending Association, "Since the occurrence of the COVID-19 virus, even with the secured product control offered by vending, it is extremely important to clean and disinfect vending equipment often, especially considering the current health crisis due to COVID-19. Fortunately, the cleaning and disinfecting process for vending equipment is easy and cost-effective. All components on vending equipment, including electronics, keypads, plastic surfaces, and glass surfaces, can be effectively cleaned and disinfected with warm, mild soapy water."[16]

Why is soap so effective against bacteria and viruses, such as the coronavirus? Soap is comprised of two-sided molecules. One side is attracted to water; the other side is attracted to fat. Viruses, such as the coronavirus, are comprised of material surrounded by a coating of proteins and fat. When viruses interact with soap, the soap molecules rip that fat coating out. Soap literally demolishes viruses in as little as 20 seconds.[17] That's why we're hearing so much about the importance of washing hands for at least 20 seconds.

There are commercial-grade cleaning and disinfectant options such as Kay 5 Chlorinating Sanitizer, which is highly effective against bacteria and fungus, and is used primarily for kitchen equipment, soft serve and shake machines, and kitchen utensils. Another option is PURELL® Foodservice Surface Sanitizer, which is an EPA registered multi-surface sanitizer/disinfectant approved for use on food-contact surfaces with no-rinse required and is currently registered in all 50 states. If you choose to use a commercial-grade product, follow the manufacturer's instructions for application and proper ventilation. Never mix these products with ammonia or any other cleanser; mixing them will cause fumes that are harmful to your health. Also, check to ensure the product is not past its expiration date. Expired products will likely not be as effective against coronaviruses.

The CDC thinks it is possible to contract COVID-19 by touching a surface or object that has the virus on it then spreading it when hands are rubbed against mouth, nose or eyes. This means that the dollar bills and coins collected from a vending machine might carry the virus. So, after handling any money it is a very good idea to wash and sanitize your hands so you don't pass any virus to yourself or others.

When it comes to the potential spread of COVID-19 through currency, some countries are taking an aggressive approach to reducing the risk of currency spreading COVID-19. China, for example, has been quarantining the country's cash. The government collected banknotes and then sanitized the stacks of bills. From there, the currency was kept in isolation for 7-14 days before being released into the banking system.[18]

The steps taken in China have not been duplicated in other countries as far as I know. However, a high percentage of your customers are probably going to change their spending habits from using cash to using credit cards. These can be sanitized as needed. Many are requesting touchless payment systems, also called near-field communication (NFC), such as Apple Pay and Google Pay. With NFC, consumers simply tap their phone to a compatible terminal such as a Greenlite, Nayak, or USAVendTech device and the transaction is complete.

"We see the cashless payment trend increasing, even while the crisis is happening, with a shift towards the use of contactless transactions. The ability to offer cashless payment capabilities encourages consumer confidence," said Carly Furman, CEO of Nayax LLC. "While the COVID-19 crisis is sure to bring unseen changes to the convenience services industry, we believe there is an underlying, long-term opportunity for operators. The current crisis may increase the growing share of cashless transactions in vending, resulting in increasing operators' profits. In fact, in a study done of 250,000 machines over an 18-month period, the number of total transactions increased by 26% on machines that allow for cashless payments."[19] Also, according to Nayax, there is a 37% increase in dollars spent when customers pay with a card versus cash.

Another advantage to credit card and touchless technology availability is that customers are more inclined to purchase more than one item from the vending machine. This is because it is so easy to swipe a card, instead of having to continuously input cash. Mobile payments don't account for much of the vending machine payments yet, but as the COVID-19 crisis continues that number will rise. So, it is a good idea to update your current equipment to have credit card readers and other cashless payment methods.

Having a credit card reader on your machine will also help you avoid losing sales due to the customer lacking cash. Along with that bonus, credit card reader companies offer access to inventory reports so you will know what you need in your inventory when you go to fill your machine.

CHAPTER 14

Next Success Steps:
Where Do I Go from Here?

Anyone who says starting a business is easy isn't being honest with you – or has forgotten what it was like when they first began. Anything worth doing in life comes with some challenges. That doesn't mean you shouldn't take the plunge.

If you're like I was and struggling to get out of bed in the morning because the job you have is robbing your soul, starting a vending machine business might reinvigorate you. There are others out there who will tell you it's an easy, quick way to make extra cash. That hasn't been my experience. What I have found, though, is I can make a very comfortable living with work that I enjoy and a business that makes me proud. For me, an appealing aspect of this industry is I can choose how hard I want to work and who I want to work with.

For so many of us, landing a corporate job was a sign of success. We celebrated our accomplishment, excited to make a difference. When reality set in, we found ourselves a cog in a dysfunctional business full of people who spent more time trying to get out of work than doing the job they were paid for. Then we stayed to please others and take care of our family.

Ten or twenty years ago, that might have been OK, but the longer you wait to find a fulfilling work life, the more hours of your life you waste. Believe me, it's not worth it.

Today is the day for you to decide to take back control of your life. Whether you decide starting a vending machine business is right for you or choose another path, I encourage to make a choice for you. Staying one more year or ten more years to get a promised promotion or reach a pay milestone is a trap. It pulls you down in other areas of your life too.

I've shared my story with you – the good, the bad, and the ugly – in the pages of this book. That's because I wanted to provide an honest guide for someone who might be concerned about taking the first step toward vending machine business ownership. My thinking is, if you read these pages and see that even I could do this, with my poor initial planning and mistakes along the way, you'll believe you can too. Of course, I also include these to help you avoid some of the missteps I took along the way.

You ought to be able to save at least two years, maybe even four, in getting your business to where you want it by following the advice I provide. I like to think everything in life happens for a reason. So, I dedicate my first two years of my floundering to you, my honored reader. You can knock that time right of the top of your business startup phase because of what I learned during those first two years – which is everything not to do.

It took me another three years to get the business to where I wanted it to be, but for the past five years, I've enjoyed a low-stress, high-reward business that gives me the freedom to do and design my business exactly how I want. You can do this too.

In the end, I've found a wonderful life that offers a relatively low-risk, stable, varied, and flexible business model. It's wonderful to have machines earning me money without the need for me to be there more than once a week. I've expanded to three geographical areas without having to add employees, by choice. I've discovered, at least in my market, manufacturing locations are the most lucrative. That's caused me to begin the shift from office buildings to hub centers and plants where I sell more with less effort.

Part of my success has been due to luck. It wasn't until COVID-19 that I realized how fortunate I was to have created such a diverse mix of business types for my machine locations. I encourage you to do the same. While others were scrambling to stay afloat, my business thrived during one of the most uncertain and frightening worldwide events of my lifetime. It pains me to think of all the heartache in the world cause by this pandemic, but I can smile about being able to weather economic chaos that has caused others to fold.

Probably the best advice I can give you is, get started! If you wait until everything is perfect, you'll never launch. Now, I wouldn't recommend you start the way I did, but you don't have to. This book gives you the basic tools to ensure you have the big research issues covered and the little details thought through before you're investing money in machines.

For many, my little 50 machine business may seem unimpressive. It doesn't matter what others think because that's what I want. I could easily expand by adding or improving locations, hiring help, or thinking bigger. I'm in my fifties now and just don't feel like working that hard. Fortunately, I don't have to because the routes I've developed pay enough to cover all my personal bills and put money aside for retirement.

Of course, your same 50 machines could be making you ten times what mine do with the right locations. Or, you might choose to only have ten and make twice as much as I do with a busy hotel focus. That's the beauty of this business. It's all up to you.

Sometimes the most valuable lessons we can learn from others are through the mistakes they've made. I've shared a good number of them related to my vending machine business already. If there's another I'd encourage you to avoid, it's staying in a corporate job too long. If you're in a toxic work environment, consider breaking free now. The vending machine industry is one you can jump into without a lot of money or technical knowledge. Plus, it's fun.

I encourage you to pursue work that will make your heart sing. For me, that's been vending machines.

If you are seriously considering starting a vending business and would like to schedule a conversation about how I might be able to help you decide and move forward faster, email me at Anne@VendingBusiness-Book.com.

References

1. Greg Sidwell, Convenience Services Industry Announces Public Health Commitment: Leading Public Health Groups Endorse Initiative, NAMA (National Automatic Merchandising Association) press release, October 23, 2019, https://www.namanow.org/convenience-services-industry-announces-public-health-commitment/

2. "What is SCORE" Copyright 2020 SCORE Association, SCORE.org

3. Tom Ziglar, "If you aim at nothing…" Ziglar On Demand, https://www.ziglar.com/articles/if-you-aim-at-nothing-2/

4. Sally Lauckner, "How Many Small Businesses Are in the U.S.? (and Other Employment Stats)" Fundora, September 9, 2020. https://www.fundera.com/blog/small-business-employment-and-growth-statistics

5. "Do economic or industry factors affect business survival?" SBA Office of Advocacy, last modified June 2012. https://www.sba.gov/sites/default/files/Business-Survival.pdf

6. Rachel Witkowski, "Banks Are Finally Sprouting Anew in America" Wall Street Journal, February 8, 2017. https://www.wsj.com/articles/banks-are-finally-sprouting-anew-in-america-1486548000

7. "SBA Loans, The Basics" SmartBiz, last modified 2020, https://www.smartbizloans.com/faq

8. "Can P2P Lending Reinvent Banking?" Morgan Stanley, June 17, 2015. https://www.morganstanley.com/ideas/p2p-marketplace-lending

9. "NAFCU Report on Credit Unions." 2019 NAFCU (National Association of Federal Credit Unions) report on Credit Unions. https://www.nafcu.org/sites/default/files/data-research/2019-NAFCU-Report-On-Credit-Unions.pdf

10. "Business Structures" IRS, last modified august 27 2020, https://www.irs.gov/businesses/small-businesses-self-employed/business-structures

11. "Apply for an employment identification number online." IRS, last modified October 13, 2020. https://www.irs.gov/businesses/small-businesses-self-employed/apply-for-an-employer-identification-number-ein-online

12. Melissa Hourigan, "Cashless Payments Grow to 37% In Vending Industry." Business Wire. June 2, 2015. https://www.businesswire.com/news/home/20150602005736/en/Cashless-Payments-Grow-37-Vending-Industry

13. Raynil Kumar and Shaun O'Brien, "2019 Findings from the Diary of Consumer Payment Choice." Federal Reserve Bank of San Francisco, June 19, 2020. https://www.frbsf.org/cash/publications/fed-notes/2019/june/2019-findings-from-the-diary-of-consumer-payment-choice/

14. "Vending Machines – A Controlled Safe Method to Provide Food and Beverages to Consumers." SelectiVend, 2020. https://selectivend.com/vending-machine-controlled-safe-methods/?utm_source=https://www.google.com/&utm_medium=organic

15. "Why Vending is the Ultimate Controlled Dispensing Solution for the Convenience Services Industry." Selectivend, 2020. https://selectivend.com/vending-ultimate-controlled-dispensing-solution/?utm_source=https://www.google.com/&utm_medium=organic

16. Lindsay Hottovy, "What Products Are Recommended to Safely Clean and Disinfect Vending Equipment?" U-Select-It, April 6, 2020

17. Brian Resnick "How soap absolutely annihilates the coronavirus" VOX, March 27, 2020. https://www.vox.com/science-and-health/2020/3/11/21173187/coronavirus-covid-19-hand-washing-sanitizer-compared-soap-is-dope

18. Jessie Yeung "China is disinfecting and destroying cash to contain coronavirus" CNN Business, February 17, 2020. https://www.cnn.com/2020/02/17/asia/china-is-disinfecting-cash-coronavirus-intl-hnk-scli/index.html

19. "Adapting Technology" Vending Market Watch, Aug13, 2020. https://www.vendingmarketwatch.com/micro-market/micro-market-kiosks-and-mobile-checkout/article/21145365/adapting-technology

About the Author

Anne Pippen started her self-employment adventure in 2010. This came on the heels of her earning a Bachelor of Science degree then logging her first 20-year career as a medical research scientist. Then she got her Master of Business Administration (MBA) and spent two years working in financial management.

Once she realized the entrepreneurial spirit was calling her, she searched high and low for the perfect small business to fit both her personal and business goals.

This search led to a vending machine business. With ambition and not much else, she started her company and the rest, as they say, is history. Anne has been enjoying the fun, rewarding and profitable nature of this industry for many years since.

Having always enjoyed teaching and helping others, Anne now shares the wisdom gained from building a successful vending business with those who want to pursue this option. If you are considering starting your own vending business, email Anne at Anne@VendingBusiness-Book.com to schedule a complimentary consultation.

A Special Bonus Gift from Anne

Now that you have read the ***Vending Business Book,*** you are on your way to starting a successful vending machine business. In this book, you've discovered how to avoid the pitfalls, mistakes and missteps that could slow you down or create financial challenges along with key information designed to help you prosper.

I want you to have a special bonus in addition to the material contained in this book. I created my *Vending Business Toolkit* to give you even more tools to help you succeed. It includes several Excel spreadsheets for tracking different facets of your business, a sample contract and a recommended resource list.

While this toolkit of ideas and forms is offered for sale, as a special bonus you can claim it for free here:

https://www.VendingBusinessBook.com/gift

There's so much confusing information out there about starting and growing a vending machine business. I don't want you to have to go through what I did to figure it out. That's why I created this book and all the additional resource tools for you to use.

I'm in your corner. Let me know if I can help further.

Here's to a solid start to a successful vending machine business!

Best,
Anne

Made in the USA
Monee, IL
15 April 2022

94780215R00085